365 Days of Infinite
Wishes & Wisdom

Ann Marie Kim

Balboa Press books may be ordered through booksellers or by contacting:

Balboa Press
A Division of Hay House
1663 Liberty Drive
Bloomington, IN 47403
www.balboapress.com
844-682-1282

ISBN: 979-8-7652-4667-2 (sc)
ISBN: 979-8-7652-4668-9 (hc)
ISBN: 979-8-7652-4666-5 (e)

Library of Congress Control Number: 2023920729

Print information available on the last page.

Balboa Press rev. date: 01/04/2024

Introduction to Infinite Wishes & Wisdom.

Infinite Wishes

Dearest Reader,

Thank you very much for choosing my book as one source to lift up your soul. I encourage you to pick up the book and open it to any page you wish. Read the message which has been written specifically in mind for you for that particular day. If you choose, you may decide to read the book each year, the message may lead you to another great book, adventure, or ignite your desire to live your Divine Life's Purpose.

I wish you love, happiness, great health, great wealth, true love, true friends and a grateful heart to soak in all the continued goodness forever.

Inspiration for Writing Book

How I came about to write this book? One day while speaking with one of the telemarketers on removing my name and address from their solicitors list, I decided to transform the encounter into one that is positive, uplifting and leaves both myself and the customer care individual soaring through the clouds.

I thought to myself, often times folks will wish you a lovely day, week or on New Years a Happy New Year, which is certainly nice. However, I noticed several decades prior while traveling throughout Europe, South America and other parts of the world for work or leisure that kindness, is, in fact a Universal language. I remember being in Paris attempting to navigate my way from the Bus station to their elaborate Train Station, even though I only had one year of French, as I showed total strangers my hotel name and address, they attempted to guide me in the right direction. As I stood there awaiting the train, a lovely young lady noticed me examining the route affixed to the wall, she spoke in perfect English and explained how she was going the same way and would let me know when my stop was. As we continued to converse, I discovered that she used to be a nanny in Newton Massachusetts, right next to the town where I grew up.

I realized that the acts of random kindness certainly 'fill my cup to overflowing'. I decided to start wishing people ' An absolutely Spectacular Life on Every level'. Depending on the day, it may be Wonderful, Excellent, Incredibly Lovely, etc. Whichever greeting/blessings/positive words they may be for that particular precious soul who has come along my path, I never concern myself of what to say, instead I am led by my heart to say a positive wish, to encourage that particular soul for eternity.

Yesterday, I attended a fund raiser for a friend here in the Twin Cities and I wished the entire welcoming committee table a simply Wonderful Life on Every level. There was one lady in particular who was visibly blow away. She pulled me to the side to thank me for such a blessing, with tears bubbling up from the core of her soul to her eyes.

My soul was basking in the happiness and love I felt from this total stranger, who on some level, has just become connected with me in this ushering of blessings, goodness, joy and positive energy to our incredibly beautiful planet.

Later in the evening, another precious soul who was the recipient of the wish sat at my table, one seat away from me. She leaned over her husband and reached for my hand, thanking me for the blessing and asked me how I started on this journey. I explained how wishing people a wonderful day, week, month, or year is nice. However, I desire to wish them a wonderful life...on every level, this is forever and everyone who hears it benefits on levels I am continually experiencing the goodness from.

She said now when she is standing in line at the grocery store, instead of complaining or talking of nothing of consequence, she is going to pass on the goodness, wishing folks a similar wish and/or blessing. I expressed my heart-felt gratitude as tears welled up in my eyes...I thanked her solemnly for sharing her intentions since this is exactly my hearts desire...to have a ripple affect of kindness and positive energy traveling all over the planet and sinking into the hearts of all human beings as a great rain soaks the soil to nourish our plants, trees, insects and wild life and eventually nourishing our souls with incredible, healthy vegetation to powerfully maintain this incredible body we each have the honor to live in.

Day 1

Today is my brothers Birthday and I am dedicating this Positive Wish to him and all of my wonderful readers, friends and "strangers" I have and continue to Wish an Absolutely Spectacular, Wonderful, Excellent, Blessed Filled Life on EVERY LEVEL. 'As you plant your 'garden of life' reach for things that lift up your soul. Phillipians 4:8

Day 2

I have decided almost 5 years ago or so to wish beautiful souls a Wonderful Life on Every Level. Today, I had the honor to speak to two wonderful individuals. I contacted my credit card company to inquire on a piece of mailing I had received. I discovered that the name to my credit card Rewards had changed and now as a customer I have the opportunity to receive even more incredible perks. I said to the young lady on the other end of the line, well, I guess the real reason for me to call today is to Wish You an Incredible Life on Every Level. I explained how the Wish/Blessing last for an eternity and that it does not matter how she may view an obstacle in her life, the truth of the matter is that she is now destined to have a Simply Incredible Life on every level. I truly love hearing the expressions afterwards. Anyone could hear the sincere gratitude in her voice, as she said Thank you so much, that is so nice. I wish you the same also. I know for certain each time I wish anyone this Wish, the Words have been spoken and become a reality in that moment. So, now you precious soul, yes, You, who has purchased my book and is reading this story. I wish the very same Wish for YOUR LIFE. I wish you, precious, precious soul, A SIMPLY SPECTACULAR LIFE ON EVERY SINGLE LEVEL. May we pass this goodness around the planet all wrapped up in LOVE. Speaking words of healing Proverbs 16:24

Day 3

Over the past month I had been experiencing water in my basement. I could not figure out why this was occurring. Although, I must admit, my higher self (we all have one) the 'little' voice that says, why not have the septic tank pumped? I responded back in my mind, I was told that I do not need it pumped for another two years. After contacting my plumbing and heating company and having an individual come over and not listen to any of my promptings of checking the sump pump or opening the lid to the septic tank, instead he assured me that it was run off water from outside coming into the old drain. Exhausted from starting a new engagement, I said sure and he went on his merry way. A day or two went by and I discovered that the water was expanding and not receding at all. I contacted my plumbing and heating company again and decided to follow the person around. This young man was exceedingly bright, he solved the mystery by doing exactly as I had requested of his co-worker (who is no longer permitted to work on my home) Within an hour and a half the young man solved why the breaker switch kept ' flipping' and discovered that the person I hired to input a pump installed the incorrect kind. I was thrilled and delighted at how smart this young man is.

Once the 'dust' settled, I realized the subliminal message, the analogy of ridding my life of all of the manure, all of the drama, all the toxic relationships, all of the unhealthy foods and to take care of my body, soul, mind and heart. Here is wishing you a life free of the manure! Clean out your closets, your pantries, your fridge, rid your home of items you have not worn or used for 6 months to a year. Rid yourself of the clutter and only purchase items that bring beauty to your heart and soul. Rid yourself of toxic romantic relationships and know that You are completely worthy of Love. You deserve to be loved by someone wonderful, who honors, cherishes and respects you. You deserve to be with someone who is committed to your relationship, who is faithful, trustworthy, an ethical and honest person who is kind, gentle and incredibly fun to be with. You deserve to be in a romantic relationship whether dating or married that only gets better day after day, year after year. You deserve to fall completely and utterly in love with the man (or woman) of your dreams and yes, live happily ever after. I am wishing everyone reading this page this Life of Bliss and more. True happiness, love, prosperity, immense good health and goodness on every single level for all eternity. Have a Beautiful Life. Love you, xoxo Romans 12:2

Day 4

Ironically, I meant to share the rest of the story of how I wished the incredibly nice lady Denise, a truly Incredible Life on every level. I wish her a Wonderful Life every time I call in for my annual servicing of my furnace, water heater and air conditioner. Yesterday, however, I felt a deep desire to express to her how important this Wish for her life is. I explained that this wish seeps deep down within the crevices of the soul, lifts up her entire being and carries her through life showering her with complete and utter blessings of all kinds. The wish is eternal and may never be reversed. I love it, I simply love wishing such incredible forever lasting goodness on precious souls everywhere. I love wishing this very same wish on your life as well, as you read through the stories of this Incredible 365 Day Journey, may the words of my heart encourage your heart and soul...,and may you pass on incredibly kind words to another. Before we know it, those incredibly kind words and endless wishes shall travel all around the world and encourage, lifting up and healing endless souls everywhere. Thank you reader for making my day today. Thank you for allowing me to reach yet another precious soul to wish endless goodness, great wealth, perfect health and happiness forever. Psalm 21:6

Day 5

Decide to celebrate yourself! If you, however, have people in your life who are nay sayers or attempt to poo poo on your dreams, decide to say, no to this person and send them away and out of your life in love. I have come to realize that you will not change the person. Today, I attended an Art A Whirl event with a colleague from work. Everywhere I go, I see endless opportunities to wish complete strangers an absolutely wonderful life on every level. The colleague told the stranger that if I did not wish them a wonderful life, I would have been bummed out. Which is not true, I choose to use positive words. Filling my life with positive powerful words that I believe resonate from my inner being, this is the most powerful place to live from on the planet for me. I believe in choosing ones friends wisely, I also learned by her responses that I should not have shared my sacred dreams with her as she listened to me speak to this stranger on how I recently invented some items. Be kind, wish people well and send those away silently in your heart in love who are not resonating at those positive levels you choose to live at. Revelations 7:9-10

Day 6

You are perfect exactly as you are. Be patient and peaceful. There are thousand upon thousands of Angels around us all of the time. Every single thing that we perceive or even desire that we need shows up in complete and utter synchronicity. Inhale and exhale deeply, fill your precious lungs with clean crisp air and release all of the toxic thoughts and any negative energy. Send those circumstances away and out of your life in love and focus on witnessing the beauty everywhere. Carving out room in your heart, life, and soul for receiving the best on every level is the first step in ushering in a beautiful life. 1 Corinthians 13: 13

Day 7

I love the definition of the spiritual number 7, which is the number of completion. What have you decided to complete in your life today? My Wish for you today is to complete one item or task you have set aside. Complete the chapter in your life that leads you to spending an hour a day nourishing your soul, for instance, finish reading a favorite book, mediate for 20 minutes, go swimming, go for a walk in nature, call a good friend to say hello, lift weights for 10 or 20 minutes a day to strengthen your bones and your mind. Complete writing a book, or a chapter or page a day. Complete your sentence of telling that special someone how much he/she means to you. Complete any item or circumstance you believe may require completing. Sit still, ask your Higher Self (which I believe is the Spirit of God) to show you what your deepest wish is, if you need to complete something. Completing any chapter in your life you may feel is unfinished, closes the door to that chapter and allows room for new beginnings, new adventures and a bright future with the opportunity to allow tons of happiness to enter into your life. Proverbs 15:13

Day 8

Romance: One of my favorite French Masterpieces is Pierre-Auguste Renoir's Dance at Bougival 1883. Each brush stroke resonates love, his true love for his wife. The gentleman holds her close and although his eyes are covered by his snazzy yellow hat, his posture and slightly flushed face is evidence of the love exuding from his heart, showing us the love he feels in his heart towards his dance partner. She, with her lovely red bonnet and gorgeous white tapered gown laced trim in gold, is truly smitten as she receives his embrace, as the two glide effortlessly across the lawn, with admirers gazing upon them, admiring and appreciating the love emanating from the two. Dance with your romantic partner, dance on your lawn, in your kitchen or in a beautiful flower filled meadow. Love, appreciate and respect each other as you glide through the beauty of your lives together.

All of my life, I envision falling head over heals in love with someone wonderful who shall dance with me similar to Renior's Dance at Bougival. My wish for everyone reading this and for those who are completely in love with romance or who desire someone special in their lives to love and to be loved by ....I wish you a completely beautiful relationship, one that is better than your wildest dreams and your deepest hearts desire. May you live a completely love filled life with your perfect match in total bliss always. Promise me this...You shall believe that you are worthy of a great, true, faithful and romantic love. You are worthy of one incredible romantic relationship of your 'tailored -made' hearts desires. Go ahead, open your arms and receive the goodness of this Wish. May God, the Creator of the universe bring you your true love. By the way, the number 8 means a new beginning. Start your new beginning with your current love, view them in an entirely different light of love, (through lens of appreciation, gratitude and Awe). Remember how you met, or if you are just in a relationship or desiring one...pay attention to these details, journal them so that you may share them later, or create a present for your significant other, with memories of each special moment, leaving details around the house, or notes, or whatever your heart leads you to do...whatever you do...love and truly respect and appreciate each other and here is wishing your love lasts a lifetime. Psalm 86:15

Day 9

Be brave and follow your heart. Decide today, instead of comparing yourself to others and possibly wishing you had their lives....start listing everything you love and appreciate about your own life. Speak words of strength, confidence and goodness to yourself. Believe in the power of God that has created you and has equipped you with the ability to live the dream He has planted within your soul before the creation of time to live now. Psalm 139

Day 10

Here is wishing you Well, Wishing you a life filled with complete and utter Bliss, Happiness, Joy, Great Health, Great Wealth and true love, true friends and true family to share the precious time we have on this planet together with. Cherish and relish in the goodness of now, of today and all of the tomorrows. Psalm 105

Day 11

Today, I met an incredible young man, I spoke with him for a few minutes. He built this incredible lego bridge which is simply phenomenal. I asked him how did he decide to build it. He said, he built the lego bridge one section at a time. Amazingly enough, he did not have a plan, he followed his heart and the businesses contacted him, he is paid by each commission assembling he creates for whichever company desires to hire him. He did not fester, worry or pursue anything. The bridge was built for Brittania and then the Genus Book of Records contacted him, everything came to him. Upon talking with him and feeling his confidence radiating out and the energy he emitted from simply doing something that he loves, I became more peaceful, realizing his experience is similar to Mozart. Mozart had dreams upon dreams where the music presented itself to Mozart. I believe my desire to hold Workshops and Seminars on line and in person in select places around the world is already aligned. All I need to do is to continue to write, complete my books, Workshop and Seminar Agenda, knowing that the precious souls who need to hear my positive messages shall show up, listen to my CD's read my books and attend my Workshop and Seminars. What an incredible truth. Live your truth now. Jeremiah 29:11-14

Day 12

One of my favorite authors of all time is the late Dr. Wayne Dyer. He often spoke about the 'Art of Allowing', trusting that the exact people and circumstances show up precisely when we are ready. Dyer quoted the Course in Miracles often, "when the student is ready, the teacher shall appear". Decide to thank those precious souls in your life who remind you to be peaceful and trust in the process of life. Similar to each bud on the trees in the Springtime, everyone knows when to show up and when to start blossoming, without any external reminders. The same is true for our lives. We each have a dream that was deposited into our souls prior to the creation of time. Practice a state of being in complete AWE. Surround yourself with nature, beauty and a peaceful demeanor and heart, allowing the people, place and circumstances to present themselves to you, all of the ingredients to allow your dream to come to life. Acts 17:26

Day 13

Positive Affirmation for life: I love life and life loves me. I love being in-love and being in-love loves me. I love walking along the seashore and the seashore with its beautiful foam loves me. The foam embraces my tender feet, shins and legs, as I glide through the salt water. I love dolphins and humpback whales and dolphins and humpback whales love me. I love and adore bald eagles and bald eagles love and adore me. Fill in the blanks, what do you love, what are you most appreciative of? Express your gratitude and bask in the beauty of the moment. 1 John 3:16

Day 14

Go to the place in your heart and from this place say, I am here to support my purpose. I am sending Divine Love into your entire being. You are completely provided for, taken care of and loved immensely in every single way. All of your needs and desires have been and shall continue to be taken care of now and for eternity. Go in peace my friend and live a completely blissful, lovely life on every level. Matthew 11:28

Day 15

Rid yourself and heart of any tears of sadness. Grieve if you choose to grieve and then decide to get up and live the gift of life you have been given. Appreciate the person, thing or circumstance that was previously in your life, list everything that you are grateful for concerning the person, thing or circumstance, and then send the situation immense love. Let go and move on, allowing space for another precious soul, friendship, thing, or circumstance to enter your life that increases your level of love. Think and be positive and believe in the absolute best for your life. Psalm 143:8

Day 16

I personally love gardening. A message from my garden thoughts today, is to plant the seed of happiness, allow the seed to germinate and watch the seed grow, extending it roots into Mother Earth, provided with enough nutrients for itself and all of the other seeds around it. Decide to plant seeds of goodness, so you may reap a harvest of love, happiness, true love, appreciation, gratitude and a heart filled with AWE. John 15

Day 17

Positive Affirmations on Writing: I love writing and writing loves me. I love speaking and just the right people show up for my lectures and purchase my books whether hard copy or electronically in droves. I am eternally grateful for God's unlimited supply of goodness and for continuing to bring these precious souls along my path that may benefit the most from the words I feel very fortunate to share with them. I am an Inspirational Speaker. I love speaking positively and positive words find and love me. Proverbs 18:4

Day 18

Take time today to play. Take time today to laugh and have fun, even if you decide to walk barefoot across your grass, or fill up a small plastic pool in your yard or on your deck and declare a pool party with yourself, or with your best friend or special friend or spouse. Have fun today and tell those who mean the most to you how much you cherish them. Proverbs 4:8

Day 19

Pick up a Mirror, or look into the mirror in your bathroom. Please, peer deep into your eyes. Notice the beautiful soul behind those eyes. Notice the pure and tender heart, maintain your gaze and share with yourself how much you truly love yourself. If you wish, say these words aloud, I love you, (insert your name here), I really, really love you. Repeat these words as you gaze into your eyes several times until you notice yourself starting to believe it. We are God's masterpieces. Ephesian 2:10

Day 20

Decide to do something today that shows your soul how much you love it. Plant a tree in your own honor. Go for a hike in nature. Ride your bike a few times around the lake, pond, park or your neighborhood. Cherish the very aspect of who you are. You are truly a gift to yourself and to the world. James 1:17

Day 21

Serenity is one of my favorite words...the word soaks deep down into my soul, into my very existence and reminds me to be.... still. There is a passage of scripture in the Bible that has and continues to be my favorite. "Be Still and know that I am God".. I wish you a sense of serenity that transcends your soul and your entire existence. Psalm 46:10

Day 22

Light heartedness is a vital ingredient to utter bliss. I wish for you this day and every day of your precious life, a life filled with close friends and new friends who are filled with positive energy and resonate at a level which compliments your level of positive utter bliss and light heartedness. Matthew 5:8

Day 23

There is a gentleman I met almost a year ago in August....I never laughed as much as I laughed with him...we have talked over the phone and shared various text over the months. I love holding hands and his hands in particular are really nice. Sometimes, when we first meet someone, we want to 'jump' right into 'relationship status'. I have decided to let go of the idea of being a couple and allow our friendship to unfold naturally, without any expectations. I have finally figured out that as long as we are on course, since we are always connected to our Higher Being, our hearts know the way and illuminates our paths. For now, he shall be an exceedingly humorous friend who I talk on the phone with. Let go and have faith. Allow God to bring the perfect person to you. What is meant for you comes to you. I discovered later through a friend of mines Facebook page that this person had gotten married, yet continued to call on the phone as though he were single. I am so appreciative that he lives in another state. I am truly thankful to God for revealing the truth to me. Be patient and wait on the Lord to bring goodness into you life. Proverbs 3:5-6

Day 24

Remember, the beauty about Life is that the Truth always bubbles to the service. If you have a person or group of people in your life who appear to be an 'energy strain', meditate on the solution or ask your Higher Self / God to guide you in the next steps with this relationship or group of people. I have found releasing the individual in love and sending them away on a spiritual level also releases me from the negative energy. Colossians 3:2

Day 25

If you are running, running, running after a romantic relationship or any kind of relationship for that matter, decide to be still and arrive at the realization to allow goodness, circumstances, situations and exactly what you need to come to you. Invest in yourself by deciding to do the inner work to allow your outer world to reflect your true hearts desire and provide direction to fulfill your Life Purpose. Psalm 46:10

Day 26

I would like to share some super encouraging words that a wonderful soul shared with me recently after wishing her A Simply Spectacular Life on Every Level. I met her at a Rick Steves seminar and shared how much I love traveling and meeting people all over the world. I love wishing souls everywhere a Wonderful Life on Every

Level. I shared how much I love writing also. This incredible precious soul, looked me in the eye as she leaned over her cane and said, "You can do it". I know you can do it, become the writer, best selling author and positive speaker you so deeply desire to be, Ann Marie. Thank you incredible precious soul for your power packed words. Thank you for speaking life into my dreams. Proverbs 18:21

Day 27

I love the knowledge of knowing that our Divine Life's purpose is inside of us and shall unfold naturally, radiating from our very being. I love the idea of not having to exert myself to have my Life's Purpose unfold. Each one of our Life's Purpose unfolds naturally, similar to rose petals opening to the warmth of the sun. Relax and trust the process of Life. Decide to fill your heart and soul with good thoughts and surround yourself with positive news, books, media. Bask in the beauty of nature or in the groves of a tree trunk. Emanate heart ripples of utter joy across the universe. Where is your beam of light heading? What areas of the planet have you made brighter just because of your existence? Matthew 5:16

Day 28

Go have fun and Live your life, decide to love yourself enough to truly Live your Life and not wait around for your friends to catch up. If you wish, decide to carve out areas in your life for new friends. Proverbs 13:20

Day 29

Embark upon your illuminated path and bask in the beauty of who you really are. Be true to yourself always and know that you are perfect exactly the way you are. Psalm 139:14

Day 30

As I look back at my 20 year old self and all of you precious souls in your teens, twenties and thirties, I share from the core of my being, relax, smile, breathe, breathe, breathe! Trust from the very core of your Infinite Soul, everything is arriving, appearing and unfolding perfectly in your life. The perfect people show up at the proper time, the career, the truly romantic soul mate relationship. Decide to rid your mind of worthless chatter and fill your thoughts with positive words, deeds and actions. Say a kind word to another soul, speak words of gratitude. For instance, whenever it rains, I offer up appreciative words such as, ' the rain is washing the impurities from the earth and nourishing the trees, bushes, grass and vegetation, or I am receiving a free car wash or I do not have to water the garden today'. I promise you, if you decide to change your thoughts, your speech, and think positive thoughts, you shall notice how your life begins to change for the better. Bask in the beauty, strength and kindness of your Creator, which I like to refer to as God. 1 Thessalonians 5:11

Day 31

Decide to speak only kind and exemplary words of others. Those who may be more challenging to love, or even like, send them God's Divine Love and healing. In doing so, you heal yourself. Exodus 23:25

Day 32

On a recent flight to St. Louis Missouri, during the on-boarding process, I wished an airline stewardess a completely wonderful life on every level. This individual completely lit up in front of me, held my arm and thanked me from the bottom of her heart. I am telling you...if you decide to say this wish to random strangers from the sincerity and love of your heart, the love and kindness completely shall infuse your soul with immense Love. During the flight, whenever she would pass by my seat, I would receive the most beautiful smile and kind gestures of whether or not I desired more water. I believe she must have shared the encounter with her colleagues because each one of these kind souls were truly phenomenal as well in their service and accommodations making me feel truly at home. As I gazed out the window, thinking of a truly special person, the airline stewardess leaned over the other two passengers and handed me a piece of paper, which was folded. She expressed gratitude for the wish and said this was a tradition in her family. As she walked back up the aisle, I opened the folded piece of paper to read some beautiful words, which a total stranger decided to share with me. Here are the wishes within the tiny piece of paper, May your casket be made of one-hundred -year old oak, and may we plant the seeds of tomorrow. I have taped this message to a precious notebook that I journal in. I shall cherish these kind words forever. Send a smile to a stranger, or if you are standing in the grocery store line, speak a kind word to the person in front of you, or behind, or simply wish them a Wonderful Life on Every Level. :-) Start planting positive seeds today! Matthew 13

Day 33

I must say there are some marshmallow looking clouds in the sky right above my home. I think a huge rain storm is settling in. I have a friend who is a pilot. Perhaps, I shall send him a text? Earlier this morning, I had a chance to call my Dad and wish him a Happy Fathers day. As usual, my Mom grabs the phone and starts talking. I gently remind her that it is Father's Day and if I may speak ta my Dad. Sometimes, one parent requires more attention than the other. If you are fortunate enough to have both of your parents still on the planet, listen to their stories, however, when it is a special day for one or the other, express the wish to speak to the one parent. Then, call the other parent back later and listen to her story. Both feel treasured and special. Exodus 20:12

Day 34

Sometimes, as we visit with our loved ones on the phone or in person, their conversation may go south.... remembering events from years ago that have occurred and remaining 'stuck' in the past does not allow us to live in the present moment and create wonderful new experiences. Decide to move on. Remember, it is not up to us to change a person, however, we may choose to speak our truth gently and remind ourselves how we are all God's creation and He loves each and everyone of us equally, without bringing up our past or others past mistakes. Share unconditional love to those in your life who may be a bit more challenging to love. In doing so, you send love to yourself. Romans 5:8

Day 35

Six months ago, I traveled back East to spend the Holidays with my family. My youngest sister insisted that I stay with her and her finance. Sometimes, you do not know how to show those who are truly special in your life how much you love them. I choose to send her God's Divine Love to heal all 'broken relationships' in her life. I choose to send kindness, goodness, happiness, prosperity and security to her soul. I choose to send her Love that takes care of her soul for a lifetime. 1 John 4:7-21

Day 36

I had the opportunity to visit with one of my best friends during the same week that both of her children were graduating from middle school and high school. I noticed that my friend was a bit stressed, having all of her family in town. I have never seen her in such a place before. So, I decided to be more positive than ever. I discovered the importance of remaining silent about the obvious unhealthy family dynamics I noticed between her eldest brother and herself. The key to sane relationships is to allow your friends to see the dysfunction on their own. This friend has not returned my text messages or calls. I wish her well and I am confident her fingers shall dial my number when she is ready. The storm has passed and she is grateful that the family member is back at his home. Decide to be the kindness you desire in the world. Decide to wear the smile you would like to see on others faces. Proverbs 15:13

Day 37

I am sending the entire planet God's Love, truth, happiness, perfect health, perfect wealth and a contented heart to appreciate all of Life's gifts. Romans 12:6-8

Day 38

I am thankful for starting a new engagement with a new client tomorrow. The business environment seems quite pleasant and I am excited to either silently or in person, wish these precious souls a truly wonderful life on every level. Phillippians 4:10-20

Day 39

Choose God instead of religiosity. Each and every one of us has an inner wisdom that has been deposited within our Soul from our Creator, of whom I like to refer to as God. Our inner wisdom serves as a barometer, illuminating our paths, if and when we decide to listen to that inner wisdom, repetitive thought, or an inner knowing, the answer to our question is illuminated. No one may live your life for you, your life has been given to you as a gift. Having said this, no one may have your Faith for you, or view life exactly the way that you do. You are special, precious and unique. Think about this, when God/Source/Spirit made you He ensured that you would possess your very own strain of DNA, fingerprints, smile, eyes, hair color. Face it, the Creator of the universe is crazy about you and desires deeply for you to take in a deep breath, exhaling, knowing that every single aspect of your life is taken care of. There is plenty of supply, abundance and prosperity for everyone. At any moment, we may choose to step out of and discard any old unlimited thoughts or beliefs and walk forth basking in the beauty of your new and renewed faith. Hebrews 11:1

Day 40

A pretty significant number, the number 40. Although, I have taken the pledge to never discuss my age any longer, after reading, watching and meeting in person one of my favorite authors, Dr. Christaine Northup (her book Goddess Never Age). I have noticed how so many of us become concerned when approaching this age. Truly, my friends, Life is what we make it. If you decide to wake up each morning and find something to be appreciative about, move your body, go for a walk in nature, or purchase a DVD to work out in the convenience and comfort of your home, then do so. Love yourself enough to truly show up in your world. Decide to take the extra half hour to do Yoga, or lift weights, squats, which ever activity speaks to your soul. You are just as precious a few decades later than you were a few decades earlier. Have fun, fill your life with laughter and friends/family who allow you to be yourself. Isaiah 43:4

Day 41

I believe we are all connected on a Spiritual level. I believe every molecule, ray of sunshine, cool breeze, each one connects us, regardless of how far away we may live from those we love or care deeply about. I cannot count how many times when I thought of my Mom, she happened to be thinking about me. I am truly blessed to have had such an Amazing loving Mother. I am confident she smiles as she witnesses my life from heaven. Share goodness with those you love, never hesitate to let them know how precious they truly are to you. James 5:13-18

Day 42

Set aside time for silence, sit quietly and observe the way the branches dance and flow in the wind, how each tree sways so gracefully against the backdrop of a perfectly blue sky with cotton ball shaped clouds drifting along as if to say hello to all of creation. Open the windows and let the fresh air into all the crevices of your home and heart. Breathe, just breathe and know instinctively everything is fine. Life is perfect and exactly as it should be. You are safe, loved and cherished by yourself (and if you have been loving yourself enough) then there is a special someone right there either beside you or showing up at the perfect time (on God's timetable, which is the best). Great work!!!! Keep loving yourself and watch this love overflow to others and all over the planet!!! 1 Corinthians 13

Day 43

Ever since I was a young girl, I had this fascination with living in the country one day. My Dad grew up on a farm and the stories he shared sounded as if he had adventure upon adventure. Believe me, I am very appreciative to have had the opportunity to grow up in a cosmopolitan city, however, I would not trade in the experience of living out in the country for anything. The wind has it's own song, naturally all the various species have their own song, dance or jig. I love bald eagles and yesterday for the very first time ever in my life, I saw a black bear up close with her cub. How amazing, what complete and utter beauty. I understand why so many people flock to the state parks to go camping. Being in nature is infectious, Henry David Thoreau understood this completely and I am so appreciative of his sharing his wisdom with the world. Go, run bare foot on the grass, bask in the beauty of nature. Take in a beautiful sunset with that special someone who makes your heart race. Love each other and be kind to everyone. Ephesians 4:32

Day 44

I am so appreciative of Doreen Virtue. As I fasted yesterday, I pulled several of her Angel cards. The one speaking volumes to my soul was the Author one. As I read the description, tears welled up in my eyes. Even though I do not believe in praying to anything other than to God, I thought it was neat that I selected this particular card. Ever since I was a girl of 11 years old, I used to walk to the library and read the magazines called Writer's . I read each new volume from cover to cover, envisioning, or planting the seed back then to become an author. I always wished to write, words are the best source of communication and writing would enable me to reach the people (like yourself) who truly desire to hear my message. I love what the Angel reference book said....simply write, decide to take an hour each day to write. Do not worry about what to say, the practice of writing opens up ones soul to allow the words to flow onto the pages. I believe each of us showed up on the planet for a specific purpose. Relax, decide to take one step at a time. If there is a desire within your soul to write, then write. Decide not to concern yourself with all of the other books that are being written or have been published...only you have the message that you need to share with the planet. Share it and choose to align yourself with the wisdom within, relax, have fun, and write, write, write. There are a couple of really neat books I have read over the years that I completely adore. One is called 'Tree Spirited Woman', the author is from Stillwater, Minnesota and at the moment her name is escaping me. I love her book, though and each time I see a red tail hawk, I remember the advice her grandmother gave her, which she was so kind to share it with the world. Whenever, you see a red tail hawk, of which I am fortunate to have a pair nesting on my property, decide to Let go, have faith and Let

God. What an incredible message from Nature. The second book, I adore is called, Letting the Divine Take the Lead, by Tosha Silver, the entire book is incredible, just as Tree Spirited Woman, however, there is one line that Tosha says repeatedly, without God maybe it will cost XXX or whatever the circumstance is she happened to be facing. Tosha shares in a remarkable, lighthearted manner how with God every single detail, details that we may have not even considered, work out before our very eyes. I believe this with all of my heart. If you have a chance, read these two books to help feed your dream, feed your soul and increase your belief in goodness everywhere. Jeremiah 29:11

Day 45

Do not Rush. Take your time, live in the moment. Pay attention to someone, hang off of their every positive word. Smile, hold the door for someone, wish someone a Wonderful Life on Every level and let them know that the wish lasts for an eternity. Then, as you walk away, know that you have just contributed to spreading goodness all over the planet and to your very own soul. Rest assured that person shall do the same. Take time to slow dance with your sweetheart, look him/her in the eyes sending them immense love without saying a word. Feel each others presence and the beauty of each others embrace. Psalm 40:3

Day 46

Today, as in normal practice, I wished several precious souls a Completely Lovely Life on every level. Two of the recipients, in particular were utterly grateful. The first individual I believe is an attorney at the client I am currently working for. As I headed to meetings, to the rest room or back to my office, this person would appear. Finally, as I headed home for the evening, upon boarding the elevator, yes, you've guessed it, this person hopped into the same elevator. I smiled and wished her a Truly Lovely Life on every level, being sure to accentuate that the wish lasts forever. My heart was touched as I witnessed her touching her heart and saying how incredibly kind and generous the wish was. (She wished me the very same Life). The second precious soul I witnessed as I headed through the sky way to catch my bus, initially, I intended to fly past her, since I needed to catch my bus on time and I had already by this point wished two to three people a Lovely Life on Every Level. I could feel this young ladies energy, she appeared to be quite sad as she gazed out the sky way windows. My Higher Self urged me to turn around and wish her this powerful blessing over her life. I followed suit and did exactly as my soul prompted me. Witnessing her shock, reaction and utter appreciation brought tears to my eyes. The young lady literally began to sob, tears were streaming down her face as she thanked me for such a wish. I smiled and said you are welcome. I wanted to give her a hug, however, I realized that these powerfully positive words, which lasts for an eternity had and shall continue to do exactly that for the young lady. As I hurried to my bus, I had to constrain the tears, which so powerfully beckoned to flow freely down my face, I felt my nose filling up with emotion and turning red, my Higher Self smiling gently to my physical self, expressing gratitude for the opportunity to witness such incredible kindness. Each one of us is very special, we have no idea how the power of our kind words, gesture may change another souls destination forever. My heart's desire is for you to be encouraged by reading this passage and only if your heart prompts you to, be the highlight of a total strangers day, year, or lifetime by passing on kindness. Philippians 1:21

Day 47

I often hear people's responses when I wish them A Simply Wonderful Life on Every Level, a large number of people share how no one has ever wished them that before. Normally, I find most lovely souls completely appreciative and many share how they intend to pass on the goodness. I am currently reading a book titled, Nothing Changes Unless You do, by Michael Robbins. I read a passage today on the bus ride home, where he expresses the importance of being gentle and kind with yourself. I love his advice here...think about it, allow these words to permeate deep into your heart, mind and soul. What does it look like in your life to be gentle and kind to yourself? For me, I have the opportunity to be patient with myself, slow and steady wins the race has always been my 'motto'. I am in the process of making better life choices for myself. I am eating healthy, choosing to walk the stairs and even when I dine out with friends, I select healthier restaurants to frequent, realizing that the menu most definitely has several selections, I may easily choose from (e.g. a fresh salad, salmon, cod, walleye dinners, or a nice organic vegetarian (almond flour based) pizza, or almond based flour homemade waffles, etc). Going for a walk in the park, going to bed a half hour earlier to ensure a solid nights sleep, enabling my body and organs to rest and start the repairing process are all expressions of self love. This past Saturday, I decided to declare a fast for the entire day. I felt great, I drank lots of ice water as I worked on my yard from 9:00 am to 4:30 pm. (Please note: I do not recommend everyone doing so, the weather was extremely hot and I had to hydrate often. If you choose to fast, decide what is best for your life. My fast was honoring our Creator God and I expressed my appreciation for my flower gardens, vegetable and spice gardens, for the beauty of the day, for all of the beautiful animals that visit my yard, for the formation of the clouds as each one danced across the crisp blue sky and anything else my heart happened to be appreciative of). For me, fasting helps me to focus and in the same instance, allows my body to rest and cleanse itself of any food impurities. I must admit, I felt so refreshed on Sunday, I did not eat anything until noon. Choose how to be gentle and kind to yourself, you know exactly what being gentle and kind really means and start living this way today. Enjoy your Beautiful Life my friends, Enjoy. Ephesians 4:32

Day 48

Belief. A very powerful gift each and everyone of us possesses. Recently, I started a new engagement and as customary I love wishing new acquaintances and total strangers a simply Incredible Life on every level. Yesterday, a young lady of whom I wished such a life long blessing came into my office and shared how the minute I wished her this wish, as she was walking towards her bus, a twenty dollar bill lay on the ground in front of her. Eyes filled with complete awe, she explained how no one was around, the streets were very empty and immediately, her thoughts raced to my earlier wish for her Life. As she shared her experience, I was inspired to start journaling the evidence of my Wonderful Life. I think this is a capital idea because then, we have actual evidence of being in the 'front row seat' of our lives and watching the goodness flow in steadily. I am amazed, honored and in awe at how grateful, thoughtful and expressive this young lady's heart is/was. I am certain she shall share even more amazing stories of which I intend to share with you. If you wish, start a journal, whether it be a written one, or a video recording or pictures. Today, I took a few pictures of the most beautiful flowers and cloud formation on my walk in the park. Which ever sends your soul soaring, capture those memories in a way you may enjoy at any time. Happy 4th of July weekend. Thank goodness for our Independence on every level (thought, heart, mind, soul, and choices). Thank you also to all of the men and women serving in our Arm Forces to grant all of us the freedom to live as we do in America. 2 Corinthians 3:2-3

Day 49

This morning, I had the day off. I slept in and then decided to balance my check book, save 10% of my income for myself and then for other interests. As I finished curling my hair, ready to head to the local library, my phone rang. It happened to be one of my dear friends who lives in town. She called to tell me news of her husband and some recents events that were not favorable for him. I listened as I picked out clothes to wear for the day and then, true to form, I gave her my advice. Afterwards, I thought, perhaps she did not really wish to hear the advice, perhaps all she needed was for me to listen. Not certain, I sent her a text and explained this and I sent a prayer stating how protected each and every one of us is at all times. I shared how I just thanked God in advance for sending her some extra Angels today to watch over her and her family. A little while later we spoke on the phone and she thanked me for all of my advice and reminded me of how precious I am. I truly believe the people that show up in our lives show up for a reason....we each have the honor to either treasure the friendship or simply walk away. There have been acquaintances that for various reasons and circumstances, I had to say goodbye to. Honor your soul, if you need to share advice with friends that may be a little much for them to hear, wait a few hours or send them an email. I have found that although friends may at times face challenging situations, they have called you for a reason and the reason normally is to seek your advice. Be good to yourself and to your true friends, speak the truth from your heart and leave the rest to God. John 14:6

Day 50

Preciousness. Beautiful sunsets, sunrises, cloud formations, a great love story, true love, romantic picnics. A lovely date with the man of your dreams, visiting your favorite quaint bookstore in a tiny little town where the food is homemade and the people kind. Happiness, a state of the heart. Sunshine, a beautiful yellow ball in the sky with warmth that causes every beautiful flower, rose, or baby tree to grow. Sunshine causes garden to flourish, nourishing our bodies, souls and lives on every level. Enjoy the bliss of Summertime. 2 Peter 3:18

Day 51

I listened to one of my favorite CD's today, "I Can See Clearly Now", by the genius, the late Wayne Dyer. He explained how every single person who comes into our life is there for a reason. It is our astuteness that enables us to recognize the reason. There is no need to 'spin our wheels' in attempting to figure out why the person is there, the infinite intelligence of the universe (which I refer to as God) shall reveal the reasons why in due time. For me, this is a very exciting way to live life...knowing that each person who shows up, there is a reason. I also listened to another favorite author, Louise Hay....she mentioned how important it is to open our arms wide and say each day, " I am open and receptive to all good and I receive it now and thank you life". (By the time I am editing this book, I have discovered that precious Louise Hay has passed away a year ago tomorrow). Yes, we all have endless goodness, if we take a moment to look at all of the good showing up in our lives. Countless evidence exists of all of the circumstances recent or over the years that have worked out for our absolute best interest. Recently, I started thinking back to how much I wished to date this one guy, it was the beginning of the New Year, he was confused and fickle. Initially, he called every single day and on the weekends he talked incessantly, then flew into town, took me out for one of the most romantic dinners ever, whisked me away to New York to a beautiful piece of land and as we went for walks each day...he would talk about the women he dated, his ex and so forth. One day, I took a walk alone and as I reached the top of the hill, acres away from his home, I lifted my eyes, arms and soul up to our Creator- God and I said I deserve the best, I deserve true love and I send this situation away and out of my life, if he is not the right person for me. As I headed back to his home, I was greeted by him in the doorway, he had arranged a flight for me to head back home the following morning. I was thrilled, however, did not want him to know just how much. I got up the next morning, had already packed the night before, had breakfast and got in his sisters car and drove to the airport. As we drove down the driveway, I looked in the side mirror, rolled down the window and waved a final goodbye. I knew within my soul that he was not emotionally mature enough to be in a relationship and I knew this was the last time I would ever see him again. He had never learned to truly be faithful, I believe, to anyone. Although, it was hard at first, I must say, after six months and now, five years later, I may honestly thank God for not allowing that relationship to sprout wings and fly. My heart and soul were spared any further drama. I am now open and receptive to receiving true love and I trust in perfect timing. Never settle and choose to believe All is well and that God is working all of the circumstances out behind the scenes. Trust and have faith. 2 Corinthians 13:5

Day 52

(Continued from Day 51) Ironically, as I conversed with him on the phone prior to then and even occasionally afterwards, I happened to speak with a customer service representative of a favorite company I purchase products from. I shared the story with her and she proceeded to share a similar story with me of what happened with her. She too thought that she could not go on and missed the gentlemen she had dated profusely, then finally, the pain went away, she, as I have, moved on with her life and a new gentleman came along. Now, she is getting married to him this month and has not thought of the other fella at all. I love happy endings and new beginnings, ladies, let's live our happy endings and happy beginnings and everything lovely in between. Ecclesiastes 7:14

Day 53

Today, I noticed beauty immediately, as I started my errands, I traveled over to a local store, purchased a foam cushion and as I headed towards my car, I noticed a vehicle which had in large letters on their rear view window, "I love you." I must admit, I do not believe I have ever seen an 'I love you" on the back of someone's window. I immediately thanked God/Divine Love for such a beautiful message. Know for certain in your heart that we are all truly loved by our Creator at all times! I believe because I have decided to pay attention, I spotted the message from above. As I sat there in my car, another persistent thought said call Walmart and find out how much their foam cushions are. After speaking to a truly nice human being, I discovered that the very same foam cushion was $15 dollars less at Walmart. I kindly returned the other and purchased the one I am now sitting on to write this entry. You see, when we decide to simplify, live within our means, God allows the universe to rise up to meet us on our journey. I believe my income is always increasing. Proverbs 8:18

Day 54

Six months ago, I made a decision to Simplify all aspects of my life. Naturally, I started with my closets and if I had not worn something for the past year, then into the bag it went. I then went through all pots and pans that had teflon on them, then any books, CD, or DVD's that I had not watched or used for a year or six month. It feels wonderful to downsize and donate items that shall be useful to others. Each time I simplify, I bless all of the items I am donating. And what is truly exciting to me is that all of those precious soul do not know they have simply been blessed forever. What an amazing concept, what an amazing truth. I love the fact that we all have the power to change our lives around for the better at any time. Like attracts like. Filling our hearts with joy, true gratitude and happiness is most definitely infectious. I love spreading those 'molecules' of love. 1 John 4:18

Day 55

As I am sitting here writing this next excerpt, I have this radiating feeling that the perfect person shall show up at the perfect time and either publish my book or assist me in doing so. I am so excited, I do not need to know all of the details. I am confident that everything I need shall materialize at the proper time. Here is wishing you the same faith, instinctively knowing that you have all that you need at every single moment in your life. Relax, take a deep cleansing breath and be Happy. Acts 17:26

Day 56

Whatever is on our mind, whatever is your biggest concern, here is wishing you relief as you place the burden down in the palms of our Creator's powerful and positive hands. Sit there, be still and allow the peace to flow into your being. Breathe, breathe again, be still, think of something or someone you love. For me, I love to think about the smell of roses or the sight of watching a bald eagle soar in the sky. Smelling, sweet, fresh roses that I have the honor to grow in my garden sends my senses soaring. I am always in awe at how velvety the roses are and no one has been able to bottle the scent into an exact replica of perfume. Isn't it amazing how the roses know exactly when to grow and when to blossom! Life is filled with the same intelligence and we have it within us at all times. This is why it is so important to be aware, here in the now and have a heart filled with immense appreciation and gratitude. It is, most certainly a far nicer way to exist on the planet. Psalm 9:1

Day 57

I am so thankful for all of the 'teachers' who have and continue to show up in my life. For each of us, there is probably someone we admire, or who may be a poster child of the road we choose not to travel upon. Take a moment to give thanks for all of these teachers and to honor your soul where you are today. Remember, life is a ripple affect, whatever we give out or decide to plant, be sure that where we are planting is rich soul (filled with happiness, kindness, respect, goodness, great health, great choices and utter bliss). A Soul possessing these ingredients reaps an incredible harvest of all of our hearts desires and more. Galatians 6:7-8

Day 58

I love logic, I particularly love watching Star Trek, Captain Kirk, Spock, Bones and Scotty, these men and the rest of the crew make decisions and solve situations constantly, I especially love Spock's logical thinking. Years ago, I was a very reactive person, until I met one of my best friends who happens to be male. I have noticed that compared to female best friends, males tend not to fret over much. This friend continued to remind me that every thing is fine, I am fine, it is all working out. Regardless of whatever the circumstances I happened to be facing. Often times, the circumstances were bigger in my mind than actual reality, over time, I found myself reiterating what he said, I am fine, it is all working out for the best. He was and continues to be particularly insightful when it comes to dating. I have dated a few duds over the past few years and I would share things with my best male friend, Instinctively, I believe because he is a guy, he knows how guys think and saved me major heart ache with two guys I dated over four years ago. Now, as I look back on the events, I must say I am very grateful that nothing transpired. One person has struggled to be employed and the other, I have lost all contact with because they drank incessantly, in the evening as we had dinner. Ladies, if you think you cannot live without this fella, do yourself a favor and take a break from him for a week, during the week and weekend, do some soul searching and create a list of what you love about this person, and then another of what you choose not to compromise with. Love yourself enough to pick the best choice. If this person is not for you, sending him away in love opens space in your life for the right person to find you. Namaste. Psalm 37

Day 59

Live simply, love deeply and laugh tons. The benefits are endless. Pslam 103:2

Day 60

Do not be afraid to 'dance in the rain', because the sun always comes up to clear up the drops, whether rain drops or tear drops. Psalm 126

Day 61

Take a half of day and just sit under a tree, watching nature busy itself around you. Listen to the songs of the birds, watch the butterflies pass by or perhaps land on your arm....soak in the beauty and be in Awe. Offer up a pleasant thought to the universe. Philippians 4:8

Day 62

I have this belief that 'walking makes me beautiful". Go for a nice walk today, it is free, does not cost a dime and refreshes ones countenance indefinitely. The Vitamin D is also very helpful for lifting our mood. Exodus 17:16

Day 63

Here is sending you the power of tons of Angels, watching over you and God guiding and providing for your every need and bestowing endless wisdom within your soul. Psalm 91:11

Day 64

Dear Reader, please know that all of these positive wishes are a wish that lasts forever, there is no expiration date for this good wish. The good wish has been spoken and manifests immediately as we live each moment of our lives. Open up your arms and receive the goodness. Yes, you, you deserve it. :-) Psalm 23:6

Day 65

Hello precious soul, have you looked at yourself in the mirror today? Have you noticed how beautiful your eyes are? How about the silent witness behind those eyes? The soul who has been with you ever since you showed up on this planet. Take a moment and tell yourself just how much you love yourself. Say, _____fill in your name here, I really, really love you. If you wish, you may start thanking yourself for all the ways you take care of yourself. For me, I am thanking my Higher self for having the wisdom to teach me how to eat healthy and to take care of the body I have. Fill in what you are thankful for, what has your Higher Self taught you today? 2 Peter 1:21

Day 66

Recently, we just lost an icon, Prince passed away a few months ago...it has affected the entire world. Sometimes, as I am sitting here watching the clouds float by, I wonder what is heaven like? Does Prince still have a chance *to play his guitar? I am sure if he can, he is rocking the Heavens. He was so generous and thoughtful to give to so many charities and great causes. I wonder if he has had a chance to meet Mozart? To me, Prince was similar to a modern day Mozart, he could play every instrument. Life is truly precious, let's decide to make the most of it, appreciating the genius in everyone you see. Romans 1:21*

Day 67

Have you ever had a conversation with God/Spirit? I believe God/Spirit loves hearing from us. Similar to how we love hearing from a good friend, family member or someone truly special. Wayne Dyer, one of my favorite authors and positive speakers has a saying that was written down and posted on his mirror. "Hello Wayne, this is God, I will be handling all of your affairs today." Thank you Dr. Dyer for being such a positive light for us, while you spent time on this planet. What a true relief for me to realize God is handling all of my affairs, always. Romans 8:28

Day 68

How are you today? Have you sent kind, loving and confident thoughts to your heart today? Have I told you how perfect you are today? Yes, you are perfect in every way, exactly as you are. You eyes are perfect, your nose, your mouth, your ears, your face, fingers, toes. You are completely perfect exactly as you are. Enjoy your incredibly lovely life, on every level. Hebrews 4:14-16

Day 69

Fill your heart with happiness, excitement, contentment, joy and a sense of adventure. Before you realize it, friends, if you are single a significant other shall appear who exhibits very similar traits. Be Positive in your actions and thoughts ....and watch all of the beauty return to you. Acts 16:31

Day 70

Today, I had visits from five or six 'walking sticks'. I am deeply honored that they chose my windows to hang out on all day. I must admit these are my most favorite bugs ever. I never knew they existed . A few Summers ago, there was a huge thunder storm and twigs, tree branches and leaves were spurn everywhere in the yard and in my entry way. As I reached for what I originally thought was a twig, I noticed small eyes on the twig and then it started to walk away. I immediately, ran inside and phoned a good friend of mine who grew up in the country and explained my new discovery. He told me that it was called a walking stick, initially, I did not believe him, (since this friend likes to play practical jokes sometimes at my expense), however, I Googled it and there was my new friend. I believe my walking stick from a couple of Summers ago had some babies, because these walking sticks are considerably smaller and green, whereas the other walking stick was larger and looked like a twig. We have so many gifts in Nature, go outside and discover which animal, bird or bug is a gift to you. Numbers 17

Day 71

I love sunsets, the entire sky is illuminated and the colors, Monet would have been thrilled over. I have come to realize that, in fact, God is the Master painter, the Master musician, the Master designer, the Master gardener and the Incredible creator. All of creation is inspired by the Master Creator. We are intrinsically pre-wired with all of our talent, interests and existence from God. Bask in the Greatness of who you are! Psalm 96:9

Day 72

Be Yourself, if there are others in your life wishing for you to be someone other than who you are, say a silent prayer for them in your heart. Bless their lives and live the Life you envisioned for yourself. Then, take each step in the direction of that vision as you are guided along your illuminated path. Cherish who you are. You are a Masterpiece. Ephesians 2:10

Day 73

Time. Spend your time wisely, because one day, you may wake up and realize that 20 years has flown by. You want to be able to look back and know that you lived it well. Carve out more opportunities to live your Life even better now. Isaiah 28:19

Day 74

If you like someone, tell them so, it does not matter if you are the male or the female. Express your heart. If you love someone, do the same. 1 Corinthian 13

Day 75

Treat yourself to a fun movie, or to the neat sweater you have been eyeing at the store. Live each day with a deposit of happiness in your heart and offer up complete appreciation for Life itself. John 13:34-35

Day 76

I believe in pampering yourself, if you choose once a month, once every two weeks, once a week, once every three months, whichever works for you...decide to treat yourself to either a SPA day at your favorite salon, or a homemade SPA day. Fill up your bathtub, light a candle and place it in a special container that illuminates hearts across the wall, place some bath crystals of lavender and vanilla in your tub and if you wish, play your favorite relaxing classical music concerto. Indulge yourself, You deserve it. Psalm 119:105-112

Day 77

Yesterday, I had the honor of completing some errands. I say honor because I believe each and everyone of us is exceedingly fortunate to have a precious Life to live. I traveled along to my favorite stores to pick up toothpaste, soap and almond flour. At each establishment I wished patrons and the cashiers an Incredible Life on every level and was sure to share how the wish lasts forever, it never expires. The cashier at the last store looked me in the eye and said, with a very gentle voice, "what a truly nice way to leave us today, especially with all of what is occurring in the world today". Initially, I did not capture everything that she said and asked her again, what did you say and she repeated it. "What a truly nice way to leave us today, especially with all of what is occurring in the world today." I smiled and said, there is a ton of goodness occurring in the world today also, and my wish is a perfect example of it. Her eyes brightened and she exclaimed and said, yes, most certainly. I encouraged her to focus more on the good occurring and more good shall show up in her life. I love my life and my very existence, it is most certainly a gift. I am honored to wish beautiful souls like yourselves reading this book, or attending the incredible Workshops, Seminars, Retreats or listening to my CD's and DVD's, a Simply Incredible, Beautiful, Fantastic, Wonderful Life on every level of your lives, and then to share how it never expires. It is my true honor to share this truth with you, "Have a Simply Incredible Life on Every Level". 1 Corinthians 10:31

Day 78

Recently, I had a couple of impromptu conversations. One with an owner of an establishment I frequent often to purchase clothing and jewelry. (Twenty-four (24%) of the proceeds is given to women in third world countries who have their own businesses, which helps feed their villages.) The second person is an old colleague. As I headed back to my car from ordering take out from one of my favorite Thai restaurants, I stopped by the establishment to say hello to the owner. She and I have engaged in some great conversations and I always love dropping by to say hello. I walked in to find her eating lunch behind the counter. She greeted me immediately and walked around the counter to visit. I shared how I wanted to purchase a fuschia colored shirt...how I intend to buy some lipstick to match. Searching through the many lovely shirts available, there was not one that was truly fuschia. She picked one shirt that had more red hues in it than pink and I decided not to purchase anything until the right color (fuschia) appeared before me. As we visited, I asked her if she had any exciting plans for the summer. To my amazement she has plans to attend a three day Workshop for $1,200 per person. Apparently, a speaker flies in from France and holds this seminar across from St. Catherines. She shared how he has relaxation classes, invites in during the meditation ascended masters from everywhere. The owner has often suggested that I have Workshops because I am so positive. I thought to myself, of course, yes. I know God/Spirit is orchestrating the details with the universe to allow one of my major dreams to unfold. As we continued to visit, she shared how she has an appointment to see a psychic. Apparently there are some major changes she is considering and needs to hear confirmation. I shared how I rely on my intuition and how this barometer never fails me. I believe our intuition is God's Holy Spirit living within us to guide and direct our steps. I love looking directly into people's eyes when I visit, since the 'eyes are the window to the soul'. There was a hardness in there that I had noticed *a couple visits prior. I immediately thought of another favorite author, publisher, Louise Hay, who shares in a lot of her writings and Seminars to gently say a prayer sending people out of your life who poo-poo your ideas. I had not completely decided upon doing so, until she shared a few more comments. Matthew 10:14*

Day 79 (a continuation from yesterday)

After sharing with her how I spoke with my sister earlier in the day and encouraged my sister to take back her power...expressing the importance of remembering that we have the power within us, (God's Spirit), to decide to change our perspective, speak positive words to our bodies, even if we may not believe it at first, continue to speak goodness to our bodies every day..and watch our bodies begin to heal, or our thoughts become more positive. Here are a few examples.

1. *Telling our body how much we love it, and "My body is experiencing perfect health now" All of my cells are working in complete and total corporation with all of the organs, veins, sinews and molecules without any assistance from medication, completely healing my body on every level.*
2. *I am loving my body and ensuring I am experiencing 8 hours of sound-full sleep each night.*
3. *I am nourishing my body with the best of vegetables, fish, and meat which is organically grown free of pesticides or hormones.*
4. *Spending time 'Day Dreaming' imagining her life exactly how she desires it to be.*

I gently reminded my sister of how she has already done this 'Day Dreaming' with attracting the perfect home to herself, bringing in her incredibly wonderful finance, living in the perfect city of her dreams.

All she needs to do is believe from the core of her being that she deserves to have a life filled with perfect health and working in the profession she desires. Wayne Dyer, Doreen Virtue and Louise Hay have always shared and even before my being introduced to their incredible writings, I have believed and still do, We are exactly what we believe ourselves to be. Jeremiah 29:11-14

Day 80 (a continuation from yesterday)

After sharing all the same advice with the owner that I shared with my sister earlier in the morning, the owner of the establishment placed her hands on her hips and said, "you are preaching to the choir, I have been doing this for the past 30 years". At this point, something in my soul told me to share this goodness elsewhere. Initially, I thought the owner was truly open to hearing such great advice, however, I felt after our conversation that she truly views me as a young kid with positive thoughts. She also expressed how she intends to see the psychic since a very trusted friend, someone who she respects their input has seen for years. Suddenly, to me, everything made sense, the hardness I would see when I looked into her eyes, even though she would attempt to mask it with a smile....the shortness I noticed one day when I was purchasing a few items in the store....she stopped wringing up my order to tell this lady if there are clothes she does not want after trying them on to give them to her. It was the tone of her voice that made me stand at attention. I wish this lady well on so many levels and am thankful to have paid attention to those nudging thoughts of the soul. We need to always remember Proverbs 16:24.

Day 81 (a continuation from yesterday)

The former colleague I mention on Day 77 called me earlier that morning. I returned her call and to my amazement she picked up. We decided since we both had a few errands to do, to talk later in the evening. I thought, perfect, I accomplished all of my errands and have the opportunity to mow my lawn as well. I love accomplishing all of my goals and relaxing for the remainder of the evening. As I took out the garbage, I pressed the call back feature and it dialed her number. She was delighted to speak with me, we visited, for a little while. I started to notice how all she seemed to do was to ask me questions of whether I am working or not. I explained how I am working at a client downtown and love the environment. We shared about many topics, which one in particular that caught my attention a third or fourth time. During previous conversations or visits with this individual, I noticed a certain sarcasm in her voice whenever I wished someone 'A Truly Wonderful Life on Every Level". It happened again last evening when I shared how someone on the bus ride home complimented me on my lovely purple shirt. Prior to the bus patrons compliment, I had wished her 'A Truly Wonderful Life on Every Level" and explained how the wish never expires, it lasts forever. As I shared this, the former colleague began to laugh and caught herself. Although, it was a brief moment, I thank God/Divine Love and the universe for orchestrating the moment to show me her true heart. On several other occasions, she had shared with a person I just wished the same blessing to, how, if I did not share this with them, I would burst or something to that affect. I later attempted to share with her how I do not use such words, nor gravitate towards such thoughts. Again, this person put up a wall of defensiveness. Then, I had my light-bulb moment....the former colleague is stuck in her own negative energy level...only when a person is ready to move to a more positive energy level, is when this soul shall accept the positive wishes. Until then, I or anyone is wasting their time and compliments to share these precious jewels with anyone who does not have an open heart. Be wise in your friendships. Proverbs 27:5-10

Day 82

I love the passage of scripture when Jesus speaks about the soil. Only fertile, receptive soil receives the water from above and grows beautiful grass, flowers, trees, shrubs. It is the same with sharing positive thoughts with people. Some precious souls eyes light up and I must say, the majority of people are truly present, living in the now, which is totally encouraging for me. These souls pause, I see them literally soaking in those positive words I just shared and declared on their lives (forever) and they normally touch their heart and wish me the very same life. I must admit, I never tire of partaking in this beautiful action. For the minor few who just nod and say thank you, I am so thrilled that I had the chance to verbally plant the seed of goodness into their souls. I know that our Creator God/Divine Love shall see to it that the seed of goodness grows in their lives as well. Have a beautiful life! Matthew 13

Day 83

Decide to embrace your life, dust it off as if you have rediscovered a precious jewel. Wear it often and bask in the admiration, appreciation, and beauty you have for your very existence. Others shall notice the glow from your being and wish to join in your happiness. Proverbs 2:4

Day 84

I love my mother immensely. Over the years, I believe it may be from growing up in a really large Italian family and being the second youngest. My Mom is an excellent Italian cook and being married to my Dad all of these years has allowed her to master additional American cuisine. Over the years, my Mom would enjoy countless meals, coupled with loving to eat ice cream late at night. I was always amazed as a child at how my mother never participated in any sports, since I loved track and field events and particularly love running. Now, in her seventies, she is experiencing leaking legs. Which I have never heard of in my life. Years ago, I would urge my Mom to go for walks with me, exercise, eat healthier foods, however, I believe when you are the persons child, the advice is not taken so readily. I talked with her on the phone yesterday only to hear her sad voice, she is wishing the doctors will give her yet another pill to fix this situation. I shared how having another pill introduced into the equation is not going to fix things. I knew that sharing about exercise, selecting healthy food choices and thinking positive would not be effective here, so I said a silent prayer for her in my heart. Then, I changed the conversation for her to share about her favorite places in Boston. It was so nice to hear her once sadden voice brighten for the next couple of hours until I had to go. Even if our love ones have conditions that we may not be able to 'physically' help them with, I am so thankful to have a chance to help,"change the channel' of their frequency or their focus and assist in directing them to share about things they love. On a spiritual level, we may send thoughts or prayers of Divine Healing, which works, in my opinion, better than any 'pill'. My Mom shared about a hot dog place, I never heard of before, however, now I know exactly where it is in the NorthEnd, across from where the old Boston Garden used to be. Jim and Nemo's . Although, I do not eat hot dogs, I intend to visit, since this is a place my mother loves and knows the owners ever since she was a young girl growing up in the West End of Boston, which is now called Little Italy. 1 Corinthians 9:24-27.

Day 85

I have met so many beautiful people over the past week or so, wishing each and every one of them a Simply Spectacular Life on every level, letting each one know, as I look into their eyes (the window to their soul); that the wish lasts forever, the blessing never expires. I am truly blessed by each persons immense thanks as I wish each soul powerful wishes of endless goodness. As I mentioned earlier, I notice that the majority touch their hearts and say thank you from the core of their being. Join me in scattering positive seeds / thoughts of goodness wherever you may live or travel to around the world. Happy Planting. Jeremiah 31:5

Day 86

Today, I visited the museum, one of my favorite places on the planet second to listening to a classical concert in Salzburg, Austria. As I walked in, I noticed a young lady in front of me, asking her significant other if he wished to view the Nature Exhibits. Immediately, I walked up gracefully, gently tapping the young lady on the shoulder. As she turned, the young lady working the ticket booth, began to smile, since she has witnessed me doing this very kindness on countless occasions. I asked the young lady and her significant other to allow me to treat them to the Nature Exhibit and both were completely blown away. On top of this, I wished them a completely fabulous life on every level and explained how the wish never expires. The love emanating from the entire encounter filled each one of our souls, either participating in the conversation or those observing it, to overflowing. I love passing on eternal goodness. It is excellent food, medicine and goodness for our souls. Genesis 41:36

Day 87

I am in the process of wrapping up an engagement and am scheduled to visit the consulting firm that just invited me to interview with one of their clients. Upon hearing the great news that I was selected from three applicants, I made arrangements to head into the consulting firm early on a Thursday morning to complete the paperwork for depositing my check, I-9's etc. As I arrived, I mentioned to the young lady the wish for a completely wonderful life on every level, she too, has a very appreciative heart and thanked me, wishing me the same. Upon completing the paperwork, she was enthralled at how positive I am and wished to inquire on how this all started. I expressed how I am in the process of writing a book, 365 days a year, for precious souls such as herself to pick up and read about all of the goodness, wishes and blessing wished and continuing to be wished for everyone reading this book all over the planet. I explained how I believe wishing these wishes are far nicer than wishing someone a great day, week or year. Genesis 49:25

Day 88

Today, I took a short trip to the Thrift Store, which is three towns over. As I unloaded my car, a very pleasant lady said hello and took the contents I was donating. As I showed her the lattice and how the clasp needed to be reaffixed, I wished her a Simply Lovely Life on Every level, again, looking into her eyes as I said each word, explaining how the wish lasts forever and never expires. Her facial expression was priceless, I almost thought I was going to start crying along with her. Standing there with her hand on her heart, she said 'thank you so much'. You have no idea what these words mean to me. What an incredible kind and beautiful wish to wish someone.' She, then wished me the wish right back, placing my hand on her shoulder I thanked her deeply from my heart. She said, I am going to need to hug you. She walked around the cedar wood lattice, I had made for my master bath and gave me a hug. I was so touched, I blessed her life even again, by saying may you be blessed forever. Everyone, we truly live on a wonderful planet, filled with love, kindness, respect and endless happiness and bliss. Smile, speak words of kindness to a perfect stranger or to those special people in your life and watch America and the world truly blossom. Isaiah 32:5

Day 89

My soul is yearning to be out in nature. I have a saying, I share with friends and family....Walking makes you beautiful. To my really close friends and family, I say, Walking makes me Gorgeous. I believe this solemnly. As we take in the beautiful terrain with the varied colors, birds flying over head, bald eagles soaring and speaking to each other in their methodical language, I am refreshed and inspired each time. I never am bored viewing all the intricacies of nature unfolding before me. Just a couple of days ago, there were two deer really close to me, just meandering in the forest. I felt so honored to be so close, watching my friends as they too, soaked up the gorgeous day. Walking is free and the benefits are endless. Have fun on your adventure! Deuteronomy 5:33

Day 90

Recently, I decided to spend the remainder of my day off visiting my favorite Indian restaurant and then walking around one of my favorite lakes. Prior to traveling to these two places, I decided to drop by a Walgreens in one of my friends neighborhoods. This particular store carries a Vegan line of lipsticks and fingernail polish. I was on a treasure hunt to find the color fuschia. Even though this particular store did not have my color, the rest of the adventure was spectacular and my favorite Indian restaurant added fish to the buffet menu. What a complete treasure. The owner promises to make Gluten Free Naan soon. How fortunate are we to have such great restaurant owners in our towns and neighborhoods. Let yours know how much you appreciate them and their fine cuisine. Exodus 33:13

Day 91

What I wish to share is the importance of nourishing our souls. If there are people, even long term friends in your life who drain your energy, it is time to look inside your heart and decide, if you think the friendship, relationship or circumstance has the possibility to change for the better. Decide to live your life with positivity embedded in each and every aspect of it. Life is way too precious to expend your compliments otherwise. Proverbs 23:8

Day 92

I have and continue to enjoy my life. I am eternally grateful for the removal of that friends drama from my life and anyone who may have the need for drama. On Friday, I had the privilege of viewing a Nature art exhibit at the museum, the experience was delightful. I met wonderful people and had the honor of giving free tickets and headsets to total strangers at the exhibit. The experience was elating. Basking in the beauty and expertise of these incredible artists (Monet, Manet, Degas, Delacroix and many others), I began to notice the intricacies of each brush stroke and the incredible detail of reconstructing the buildings in Venice. I delighted in enjoying a lovely salad from the Cafe along with their exquisite almond flour cookies. So rich and moist. The day was simply perfect. I truly believe as we carve out time to indulge in the activities we enjoy, we are truly nourishing our souls. The experience and journey become so much richer, enabling my heart to overflow constantly with immense gratitude to have time to appreciate beauty on every level. Especially, time spent in nature whether on a canvass or in my favorite State Park never fails to revive my soul. Go ahead, Bask in the beauty of life. Psalm 97:11

Day 93

Sometimes, you may find it challenging to walk away from relationships that have been a major part of your life. However, I am here to express that it is so gratifying to remove yourself from the drama. One of my favorite things is to clean my home, the feeling after ridding my home of dust bunnies and Simplifying as my favorite author, Henry David Thoreau has expressed, provides me with a feeling of relief and lightness. Clearing away toxicities of every kind empowers us to live the incredible Life we were all destined to live (for however, this may look for you). Simplify, bask in the goodness of it all and live happily, removing all levels of drama from your life. Isaiah 54:10

Day 94

I just had the honor of watching an episode of "Cooking with Julia" Master Chief series. Lidia demonstrated how to create an incredible risotto and another pasta dish that looked scrumptious. Toward the end, there is Julia, Lidia, and her husband, along with other family members in Lidia's kitchen, sitting around the dinner table enjoying some of the best Italian cuisine on this side of Italy. As I watched the lovely gathering, my heart warmed at the site of Lidia's husband playing the Accordion. The two of them signing Italian songs on either side of Julia, who was beaming with delight looking up at Lidia from her seat, signing along. One of my favorite quotes from Julia Child, is to "marry someone you love talking to". As I watched Lidia with her husband and family, it is obvious to see that she has certainly married someone who loves her dream as much as she loves his. If you wish to marry, marry someone who you love to talk to, love spending time with and who you love period and may see both of your dreams transpire. As the years pass, your hearts shall become even more knitted together, in love. 1 Corinthians 13

Day 95

I must admit, I love Louise Hay and all of the incredible authors she has on her radio station and Hay House Now. Earlier this morning, even though I own a copy of ' The Secret Pleasures of Menopause', I listened to the audio version. Dr. Northrup, in my opinion, is a gift to women all over the planet. I love listening to her 30 plus years of experience on Women's health, and her expertise on a topic that is largely shunned by most Women in America and in other parts of the world. Eating healthy, being in touch with who you truly are and removing unhealthy foods, people and circumstances from ones life and deciding to follow ones bliss, sets the stage for a most beautiful transition into the years after 50 or whenever a women experiences menopause. I encourage Women all over the planet to read and /or listen to her book, it is most liberating and provides much needed information of how we truly begin to live at this point in our lives. Even if you are no where near menopause, or peri-menopause, being educated beforehand equips one with a certain sense of empowerment, one that enables you to live fearlessly, creating, experiencing and living a life that is truly genuine to you, alone. I am completely thankful for Dr. Northrup and find her words in her book, Goddesses Never Age, true for my life. The only time I experience any discomfort in my body is if I had starchy, gluten laiden foods, or unnatural sugars. As my diet becomes filled with clean energy burning foods, my body flourishes with energy and any swelling from the gluten disappears. I believe we are all very fortunate to have such knowledge shared with us from a Women's perspective, let's face it, she has the same piping as we do and knows our bodies very well. Thank you, Dr. Northrop for allowing Women everywhere to celebrate this beautiful transition in life of becoming more authentic, more centered and in tune with who we really are. Following our bliss each day and removing the images or messages society has on this incredible transformation is the best 'medicine' for Women everywhere. I also love the advice for men in your book. Read on gentlemen. I Corinthians 15:44

Day 96

I love sharing kind words with people wherever I may travel. Yesterday, I volunteered in my local county to test the voting machines for the upcoming Primary and General Elections. As I checked the machines, by inserting some test ballots, one of my friends had left the container to the machine on the chair next to me. My leg was scrapped by the clasp. As one of the nice ladies from the county auditors office brought the first aide kit to me, after already washing the area, I applied some antiseptic ointment on it and a couple of band aides. Then, as if my soul is naturally attuned to wishing lovely souls this wish, I wished her an incredible life on every level and expressed how the wish never expires, it lasts forever. Giving the wish and having the honor to witness or hear the expressions of gratitude never becomes old for me. My soul soars in the goodness of the entire experience and although, I may not have had the opportunity to speak with you (the reader) directly...... I WISH YOU A SIMPLY SPECTACULAR LIFE ON EVERY LEVEL OF YOUR LIFE!!!! (in every area, in every way and know that this beautiful wish lasts forever.) I believe, "Life becomes better and better and better." John 14:6

Day 97

Decide today to be true to yourself in every way. Be kind, look for the beauty in every situation and create bliss in your life on every level. Choose at any time happiness above anything else. You'll discover as you choose happiness and a positive demeanor, life starts to provide more of the same treasures, endless goodness showing up on every level. I am venturing through this day appreciating the sound of the bald eagles calling to each other as I have my windows open finally enjoying cooler temperatures after a long heat wave. Bask in whatever allows your Soul to Sing. Soar!!! 2 Samual 22:11

365 Days of Infinite Wishes & Wisdom | 31

Day 98

Yesterday. I treated myself to a SPA day. I sent Divine Love ahead of me for my botanical hair treatment, hair style and for my facial. I had the best treatment and was thrilled to see the immense gratitude on each young ladies face as I wished her a wonderful life on every level. One young lady who administered my facial, my soul felt the need to place my hand on her shoulder, and look her straight in the eye to share this blessing. Her eyes welled up with tears as she expressed how powerful those words are. As I traveled along the day going grocery shopping I shared the same wish with so many people and the varied responses served as food for my soul as well. Each person expressed exclamations such as, " those are the nicest words I have every heard, thank you so much, I wish you the complete same. " One really handsome blue eyed gentleman filling the onion and potato section in the store greeted me, naturally, I wished him a Wonderful Life on Every level. You should have seen his expression, it is true, words have a powerful affect on people. His eyes widen as he stepped back, as if he took it in a huge wave of positive energy, saying Wow, what a wish, thank you, I send it right back to you as well. I am so grateful and appreciative to be an agent of sending positive words or rather planting positive words in precious souls all over the planet. I am thankful to our Creator God for placing this desire in my heart, scattering seeds of goodness everywhere. Forever! Join me in spreading kindness, a smile, a helpful hand or a kind word to anyone in your life or who comes across your path. Have a simply spectacular life on every level, always. Philippians 4:8

Day 99

Today, I intend to list all of the things I am thankful for over the past several days;

1. *The sound of bald eagles calling to each other in nature and outside my window.*
2. *The sight and sound of a red tail hawk soaring overhead, reminding me not to worry about the details of my life, everything is working out perfectly. Basically, to let go, believe and let God.*
3. *My one male best friend, Thomas Maxwell Boyce.*
4. *The consulting firm I work with JP, he is one of the most kind, professional and considerate individuals I have the honor and privilege to work with and represent.*
5. *Watching episodes of Julia Child. Cooking is a piece of art, creating masterpieces.*
6. *My beautiful new hair due, so easy to curl due to the exquisite hair design/cut.*
7. *The incredibly beautiful day and the nice gentle breeze.*
8. *I love having my teeth cleaned and I am heading to my dentist today.*
9. *Inhaling the beauty of the Nature Art exhibit at the museum.*
10. *The beautiful encounter with the deer almost coming up to me and the doe also.*
11. *Witnessing a doe sneeze.*
12. *Great conversations and excellent art fairs occurring over the next several months.*
13. *Helping at the primaries and ensuring the voting machines work.*

14.	*Living each day and having conversations with God on how incredible He is and the incredible beauty of the planet.*

15.	*My love and appreciation for dolphins and humpback whales.*

16.	*The Boston Sky line.*

17.	*Seafood chowder*

18.	*The Fisherman's Feast on Hanover Street in Boston.*

19.	*Cool breezes on a picture perfect day in the country.*

20.	*The sound of the ocean waves crashing along the seashore.*

21.	*The smell of the ocean breeze and the sound of seagulls fetching french fries.*

22.	*The sound of my mothers voice singing, Oh Sol A Meo,*

23.	*The aroma of a wild rose.*

24.	*The Angel Number 444, Doreen Virtue's book Angel Numbers, means Angels are all around you, everywhere. I love the way Angels and God speak to us.*

I encourage you to do the same. Create a list of all that you are thankful for and frequently review it as a reminder of how blessed you truly are. Genesis 1:1

Day 100

Wow! There is something about the number 100 that is exciting to me. I love the fact that for 100 days, I have had the privilege to write down and share with you, the reader, all of the lovely wishes and life lessons to assist you in creating and carving out a life of utter bliss and happiness for yourself, which naturally has a positive affect on everyone else in your world. As I sit down in my sacred space to write this morning, the words 'Infinite Wishes' came to my heart. Excellent name for the title of my book. I love the way life unfolds, as I waited for my computer to turn on, a 'teenage' bald eagle flew by my windows, I followed him/her from window to window watching as she/he ascended higher, allowing the currents of the wind to do the 'flying or navigating' for him/her. As I watched this profound majestic creation, I basked in the beauty and strength of it's freedom, it's ease of movement and the natural instinct to rise up from it's nest and fly. I viewed the sky in search of its parents, no other eagle in sight. In our lives, it is important to follow our dreams, do what instinctively comes natural to us, even if there is no one else in our lives who wishes to join us on our adventure, quest or dream. One of my favorite authors, the late Wayne Dyer talks of having the 'end in mind'. For my life, I already envision a long line of precious souls awaiting to thank me for creating the Workshops, Seminars, Individual or Group Sessions, Radio shows, Youtube Channels, DVDs, CDs, ebooks and books I have written to help inspire them to start living the life they have dreamed of. I envision being eternally grateful to have the honor to play such a role in so many lives. To share how each and everyone of us has the power embedded in our soul to change our lives for the best at any moment. Kindness, goodness, happiness and miracles occur at all times within every second in our universe and we all have the opportunity to witness this, participate and share about it with others. Similar to having the opportunity to vote in our country, we have the opportunity to change the things we pay for or give our attention to. I have been clearing and cleaning out my home, anything I have not used for a while has been donated, new items I may have purchased and never used have also been donated or given to good friends who liked the item. Today, I intend to light a candle to send all of the toxic thoughts, conversations and energy which may have accumulated over the years inside my home, out. I wish you a life filled with goodness, clean fresh air and toxic free energy. Galatians 5:1

Day 101

Clearing the space and saying an affirmative prayer (Thank you God/Spirit/Creator) for filling my home with love, kindness, beauty, great conversations and friends/family who only have my best interest in mind), creates the positive infrastructure or foundation for our souls to thrive in. As you practice focusing on the life you desire and living in a manner that already realizes these dreams and goals, your life shall begin to follow the inner blue print of your being. All of Life aligns to allow you to live your dream, your Divine Life's purpose. Live a life of bliss and happiness, decide to eliminate all moments of feeling lonely or fearful about your life or future or dating someone. Tap into the Power that has created the universe. Know with certainty that your life is important, you are priceless and must take the time to nourish your soul first in order to even begin to have any real and meaningful, lifelong friendships or relationships. 1 Timothy 4:6

Day 102

What does it mean to nourish yourself? Recently, I decided that I am only intending to eat in moderation. As I sit down to eat, I am present in that moment. I notice the food, the smell, taste, and texture. I now notice when my stomach is beginning to feel full and I no longer eat to the point of feeling uncomfortable. Even as I sit there watching one of my favorite shows, (Andy Griffin Show, Star Trek or Tattle Tales or Richard Dawson's Family Feud) I no longer eat mindlessly. If I find that I am still craving something, I fill my lovely thermos with ice cold water and replenish my body, hydrating every cell, which allows the cells to eliminate any toxic matter in my body. The second major benefit is fitting into my favorite jeans, or marveling at how one of my favorite dresses fits looser. These experiences are true gems to ones soul and adds immensely to our sense of well being, satisfaction and excitement for life. Whatever you wish to change or improve in your life, set aside 5 minutes a day, or increase the time as it suits you and your schedule. Start living your dream. Decide to no longer compare yourself to others or 'what society' deems as the norm. Find your niche and what makes your soul soar and live, simply live. You most definitely have the knowledge, instinct and ability to start living the life you imagined. I am truly happy for you on every level, as you embark upon your new journey. Philippians 4:4-8

Day 103

Lately, I have been noticing license plates that have the letters MVE on them, I ask myself is this a message from God/Spirit or the universe to move? I believe if I am to move, then my path shall be illuminated, I have a deep desire to assist in the preservation of bottlenose Dolphins and Humpback whales. I would love to live by the ocean to partake in this work. I have come to realize that once a seed has been planted, this seed of working with bottlenose Dolphins and Humpback whales (with bald eagles and red tail hawks flying close by) I know that God/Spirit allows it to grow and as I am prompted in my heart ... the next steps to take, similar to moving to my home here out in the country, the people, places and events shall occur. I read a tea bag message once that said, 'What is meant for you, finds you." These desires, I believe were already planted in our souls prior to showing up on the planet. The roadmap reveals itself when we are ready and have acquired all of the necessary life ingredients we need for the next level . Pay attention to the roadmaps and live your exciting adventure. Mark 4:15

Day 104

I love having the opportunity to show the Creator of the universe how I believe in God/Spirits power. I have a lifetime of events and circumstances to refer to, which shows me how well I am provided for and thoroughly taken care of. One of my deepest desires was to purchase a home in the country, surrounded by trees, with bald eagle nests on my property with very kind and considerate neighbors and a quiet environment to provide the space for me to write. As I reviewed the affirmations I wrote almost 10 years ago now, I realize that even more than I asked for has unfolded. The beauty and experiences living in my dream home, growing my own fruits and vegetables and soaking in the beauty around me is simply exquisite. Write down the things you truly love and start seeing yourself living the life you have mentioned in your affirmations, offering up immense gratitude along the way. I love writing and sharing positive words, wishes and stories with complete and total strangers and now my family of readers. I believe that if you have a book inside of you....sit down and start writing. Initially, I was a little overwhelmed at the mere thought of writing an entire book, however, another of one of my favorite authors, Doreen Virtue said that she writes for an hour each day. I thought to myself, an hour a day seems manageable, I may do this easily, especially on the weekends and this is how I started and completed this book for you. I wish each and everyone reading this book a life wrapped in the beauty of your realized dreams and wishes, with you stating that 'My Cup runneth over', with tears of joy overflowing in your eyes, heart and soul. Psalm 23:5

Day 105

A few days ago, I had an opportunity to wish a few lovely souls a wonderful life on every level and I must admit that I never tire of seeing the sparkle in their eyes and the way their souls literally light up as he/she may hear these words. I am thrilled when I realize that the person I wished these words to, actually showed up mentally. Sometimes, as I am wishing someone a wish, they are on automatic pilot and think I am wishing them a nice day and continue to walk on. People who are truly present take a moment to stop and listen to the words. I believe this is a perfect example of Source/ Infinite Wisdom/God placing the right person along my path to allow me to plant that wish of goodness and a gentle reminder to me to be present in the moment. So, the next time you are walking along, if you are shy at first, you may freely wish the person a wonderful wish in your heart as you pass by, or if you wish to say, excuse me Miss, or Sir and wish them an incredible life, you shall experience the joy and honor of changing someones life for eternity by simply speaking positive words into their being. As you do so, you shall automatically place positive experiences in your soul as well and spread happiness to the planet. Happy Living. Acts 17:26

Day 106

I lit a candle and walked through each room of my home, including my basement, removing all negative energy, conversations or talk or experiences from each space. The powerful affirmative prayer included any energy from previous owners or renters or anyone living or visiting this space who may have missed the opportunity to share positive words in this precious living space. I must say, it feels wonderful to clear the space and allow only goodness, happiness, joy, positive thoughts, words and experiences to dwell here now. Do yourself a favor and clear your space today. Decide to place only wonderful thoughts, experiences and conversations in those walls that envelope your life. John 10:10

Day 107

I am going to join Rodney Yee in a Yoga DVD and center my soul. I especially appreciate his videos as he provides great explanations on breathing techniques and the benefits of each Yoga pose. Yoga twists for example is designed to release all the toxins in your body's organs, I love knowing that my organs are also benefiting from this ancient Yoga practice. Choose your favorite form of "moving your body' and carve out time in your schedule to participate in that activity often. Psalm 84:2

Day 108

My heart has been drawn to meditating lately. Today, I intend to focus on one thought and meditate on this for 10 minutes or more. The thought of (I am perfect exactly as I am or Life brings to me only beautiful encounters and experiences). Focus on one positive truth/thought that resonates with your soul today Trust and Believe all of the details are unfolding perfectly, even better than you imagine. Similar to putting puzzle pieces together, of which I do often. For me, working on the outside of the puzzle, or 'having the end in mind', I fill in the pieces until the entire puzzle is assembled. During the process, my mind wanders, thoughts come easily and effortlessly. A sort of ebb and flow, similar to the ocean's tide, the knowledge I need stays and any chatter or foam is drawn back into the ocean and absorbed. Psalm 4:4

Day 109

Bask yourself in nature today, walk along your favorite path, feel the breeze on your face, notice a beautiful butterfly, or dragonfly. Say hello to the beautiful trees that give us the incredible oxygen we need to exist. Give a tree a hug, if you wish. Thank the beauty of the meadows and the wild flowers for greeting you today. If your adventure takes you to the water, thank the fish and river insects and animals for existing. Thank the atoms and molecules for adjourning together to create the wonder called life. John 3:3-8

Day 110

Say goodbye to a closed door, when it is time to say goodbye. Do the same for someone who was a friend, who happened to drain your life of tons of energy most of the time you spent visiting with them. Learning to say goodbye within your soul, releases you of the toxic or selfish energy and enables you to usher in new positive friends who actually become true friends. A true friendship consists of both parties being there for each other, walking side by side in the adventure and gift called Life. If ever, you notice that one or a few people leave you feeling drained at the end or during a visit, or you hesitate to even pick up the phone when he/she calls and if this friend consistently illicit behaviors of talking incessantly for an hour about his or her's own life without giving a thought to how you are, then, this is the type of 'friend' that is not truly a friend. Wish him/her well in your heart, however, start to reduce and finally remove yourself from their company. By doing so, you allow your soul to be restored back to a healthy state of mind, granting yourself the opportunity to attract new friends who are on the same wave length as yourself and who truly know how to be a good friend. Namaste. Go in Peace. Mark 4:39

Day 111

Bask in the Beauty of Silence. Turn your volume on your phone off for a day. Invest in yourself and the beauty of the time to yourself. Read and respond to all text, emails and voicemails a day later or two days later if over the weekend, or even if it is in the middle of the week. So often, we pack our schedules and are tied to our phone and emails. Observe Nature, everything unfolds naturally, for example, notice this Spring how the buds arrive on the tree branches or bushes in a non-rushed manner, budding at the precise time. Now, in order to stay mindful, tell your soul to witness the full unfolding of a particular leaf on a tree. I attempted to do this one Spring and before I knew it all of the leaves were fully grown on the trees. I shall make a special effort to start slowing down enough to notice the beauty of a leaf or rose bud unfolding. Nature is immensely beautiful, Live your life the same way, in utter beauty, unfolding slowly as your soak up all of the goodness in each step of your journey. 1 Kings 19:7

Day 112

Gracefully, bow out of endless invitations, declutter your calendar and only schedule time for events, people and places that you utterly enjoy. Decide to spend your time with friends and family who allow your Spirit to soar, minimize time or eliminate all entirely those individuals who may be a drain on your energy. Nahum 3:14

Day 113

A few minutes ago I had a phone call with my airlines. After receiving the best customer service from the young lady on the other end of the line...l asked her for her undivided attention, asked her to take a deep breath and to listen to the wish I have for her life. I wished her a completely Incredible Life on every level, explaining how the wish pertains to every area of her life, the wish only enables her life to get better and better, never expiring and lasting forever. She was so touched by the wish, I could literally feel her smile through the phone as she thanked me continuously for such a beautiful wish. I assured her that she is welcome and hung up my phone knowing that I had the opportunity to add more good on a Soul level to the planet. Proverbs 16:15

Day 114

I am completely appreciative to Source/God/Divine Love for the privilege to share such goodness everywhere. There is no cost to sharing this goodness and the ripple affects are absolutely amazing. Ecclesiastes 10:12

Day 115

Enjoy your own company and carve out time for Day Dreaming. Imagine your life exactly the way you wish to live it in your minds eye. Live each day with a heart overflowing with gratitude for all that you have now and all that shall show up at the perfect time. You'll begin to notice your life improving and start seeing all of the good and blessings showing up constantly. I am in Awe of all of the goodness everywhere. Genesis 41:11

Day 116

One of my favorite authors Louise Hay has a saying, Let things come to me. I started living this way and allow friends to contact me, or circumstances to present themselves as I think about the event in my mind. I love witnessing how it appears in real life. Think Beautiful thoughts as you create your world of beauty. Psalm 48:2

Day 117

Are you aware of how our bodies have been created to heal, restore and continue in strength and wellness automatically? I am reading an Incredible book 'Women's Bodies, Women's Wisdom', written by one of my favorite authors, Dr. Christian Northrop. Instinctively, I knew that our bodies would compensate for the various transitions our bodies undergo. From puberty to young adulthood to middle adulthood, to fabulous adulthood - Yes, you read the word correctly, Fabulous. Each person, especially, if you are one to eat healthy, partake in moderate exercise, four days or more a week and truly cherish who you are....may live a healthy, long, happy, sexy life. Remember, we are what we believe ourselves to be. And you my friend are handsome (if a gentleman) and gorgeous (if a woman)!!!! John 10:38

Day 118

Believe in the power that Created You. The Wisdom of the Ages which lives in each and everyone of us, knows exactly how to take care of what He/She has created. Be certain to read the labels of the food you choose to *consume, the less ingredients the better. Consuming vegetables, fruits, legumes and fish in it's natural form, minus any hormones or pesticides adds longevity to your life. Be the person who takes care of you. Become the educated consumer, even as it pertains to your health and well being. If you need to eliminate certain foods, (junk food, sugars, etc) from your life, then Love yourself enough to do so. 1 Kings 1:17*

Day 119

I recently decided to change my life even more for the better. I have eliminated all candies and sugars. I am only consuming natural sugars such as Molasses, or in some cases pure honey. Potato chips not made with coconut oil have also been removed and replaced with fresh organic fruits and vegetables, or handmade sweet potatoes potato chips with olive oil. Ironically, I do not even crave the unhealthy alternatives and on occasion, when I think I have and consume something, the candy, or chips tastes empty, which are filled with a heap of sugar or salt. I find the consumption not satisfying at all. I am so happy my body is appreciating all of the healthy choices I am partaking in now. The benefits and 'return on investment' to such a healthy lifestyle are endless. Psalm 103:2

Day 120

If you have not already, decide to have a yearly physical, have your blood checked to ensure you are eating a heart healthy diet. If there are areas you need to improve upon to reach your heart healthy goal, decide to embrace the goodness and in your heart, thank our Creator for providing you with a doctor who cared enough to order blood work. Be kind to yourself, speak positive words to your soul, as you embark on the journey of good health. Be patient also, knowing that one step at a time, one positive action at a time, allows you to reach your desired outcome. Choose healthy, happy living. 1 Timothy 6:19

Day 121

Do not be afraid to Dance in the Rain. Literally and through life's perceived storms. Truly, if you look closely at your life, you shall notice that you are very fortunate and have an abundance already. As you travel throughout your day, your life, take notice of all that you are truly appreciative of. If it happens to be a person, let him/her know. If things and circumstances, express your gratitude to our Creator or express appreciation in your heart. John 14:1

Day 122

All of Life comes together as a beautiful Dove's tail. Decide to go through your journey with minimal to no complaining or criticism of yourself or others. Fill your heart, mind and mouth with positive thoughts, words and actions and watch in utter amazement at the harvest you shall reap as a result of the positive seeds planted. Zechariah 9:17

Day 123

I am amazed at all of the different species of Whales. The Big Blue Whale is the size of a 737 airplane, the Humpback whales are known for being very acrobatic in their search for food and leisure in the sea, grey whales are bottom dwellers, eating the fungi and seaweed from the bottom of the ocean floor. There are even different whales in Brazil and the Dominican Republic. All simply amazing and fascinating. I am in complete Awe. What are you in Awe of today? Job 25:2

Day 124

There are countless species of dolphins around the world as well. Isn't it wonderful to be included in such variations of creation. Life is truly beautiful on every level. Bask in the bounty of the countless species and support a pod of dolphins today. (even if by sending positive thoughts to the ocean and all of the inhabitants and the citizens commuting across the seas). Psalm 65:11

Day 125

You are beautiful, (handsome if a male), You are very intelligent, you are charming and fun. You are precious and loved immensely. You are perfect exactly as you are and truly loved by our Creator. Hug yourself and look into your eyes as you recite these words to your precious Soul. Have a simply Spectacular Life on every level. Forever. (while editing this day, I just heard the sound of a bald eagle, how incredible) Job 39:27

Day 126

A month or so ago, we were experiencing intense thunder storms that may or may not have formed into a Tornado. My area was under a Tornado watch and I prayed for God to send His Angels to protect my property. As I finished my prayer I peered out my window in the direction of my chicken coup and noticed a beautiful cloud formation. I snapped a picture with my phone and sent copies to friends and family. Later, as I viewed the pictures, I noticed how the cloud is shaped in the form of an Angel, with her arms spread open protecting my home and property as well as all of my neighbors. Above is a copy of the pic. Simply amazing. I am truly grateful, humble and appreciative that the Creator of the universe listens to my prayers (all of our prayers). Isaiah 31:5

Day 127

I believe we all have Angels assigned to us all of our lives, from birth. Thank God for your Angels today for watching over your life and being with you every step of the way. Matthew 18:10

Day 128

As I traveled through the Uptown Art Fair yesterday, I had an opportunity to view some incredible talent. As I felt led, I would stop and wish the Artist or complete strangers who happen to walk past me or stop and talk really close by, A truly wonderful life on every level. A particular encounter warmed my heart, see Day 129 for the story. Share kindness always!!!! 1 Chronicles 29:7

Day 129

As I wished two ladies the blessing, one lady asked me to please repeat the blessing to her slowly. She expressed how my words were the most beautiful thing she has ever heard anyone wish another. As I started sharing my wish for her and her friends life, five more of her friends approached as I said, 'I wish you a completely Wonderful Life on every level and this wish applies to each and every area of your lives, which only gets better and better and never expires.' The beautiful soul almost cried as she stood there with her hand over her heart. She then asked if she could give me a hug, since this is exactly what she needs in her life right now. She and her friends expressed how much we need these words and people like myself on the planet. I must say, I am appreciative of having such souls like her and you wonderful reader on the planet. Thank you for deciding to show up. 1 Thessalonians 5:23

Day 130

My entire experience walking through the Art Fair was an incredible journey of spreading positive love everywhere, which acts as a ripple affect all over the planet. One gentleman approached me as I viewed his art. He said, I came over because I can feel your energy. He exclaimed that my energy is so positive that he could literally feel my presence in his exhibit. We talked at length of the importance of sending these positive wishes throughout the planet. As we talked further, he started to say how, he and I were the only two who were sending this positive energy out at the Art Fair, I reminded him of how the very same thing may be occurring at the very same time at this Art Fair or anywhere around the world. Kindness begets kindness and acts as a ripple affect, filling the hearts of everyone everywhere. Luke 6:35

Day 131

Kindness opened doors and orchestrated wonderful people to show up in my life as I traveled throughout Europe for work. Once while traveling by train from Brussels to Paris, I was not certain if I were heading in the right direction for the train and then on the right train to my hotel. To my utter amazement, a very nice young lady, who spoke perfect English and who happened to be a Nanny in Boston, Massachusetts for four years sat down next to me on the bench as I awaited the train and asked if she could help me . (I was born in Boston, Massachusetts and grew up in New England). A perfect example of kind souls everywhere. She showed up at the precise time and happened to be traveling to the same stop. We became really good friends and whenever I visited Paris or she America, our homes would be opened to each other. There are literally wonderful people everywhere. Isaiah 28:29

Day 132

One of my favorite authors, the late Wayne Dyer shared this one perspective a ton in many of his writings or speeches. Basically, whichever way you view your neighborhood, neighbors will be exactly the type of neighborhood and neighbors, experiences you will have if you move to another place. You see, the experiences in Life all depends on our perceptive. Have positive ones and watch your life blossom attracting new, exciting and integrity filled, brilliant friends shall appear. Psalm 19:8

Day 133

I am certain that the majority of us, if we have lived on the planet long enough, realizes that we may only change ourselves. Regardless of how much I wish to have a wonderful relationship with all of my family members, equally, I am learning to cherish who they are. Sending God's Love to each one of them fills my heart with Joy knowing that they are taken care of on every level. Stepping aside and allowing each one to be who they are without any conditional constraints, allows my heart to be free of expectations and provides more time for me to focus and manifest the people, places and events in my life that I desire. Whoever is meant to be in your life shall show up at the exact time and place. Decide not to fret over anything, instead use your energy for focusing on positive thoughts of happiness, bliss, fun experiences and laughter. James 1:17

Day 134

I have spent the last seven (7) years in a career as a professional consultant, working with really neat clients. The majority of the audit engagements have materialized through five or more consulting firms. Two of the five consulting firms are in my opinion, God sent and have been a true delight to work with. At times during those years, my focus strayed slightly from positive thoughts and I had created working conditions with some colleagues I prefer, now, not to have known. I discovered first hand, as I changed my thoughts to ones of unconditional love and sending these folks away and out of my life in love; wonderful new consulting firms appeared, who kept me exceedingly busy with great clients. My soul is leading me to work for myself now....and although I am a little nervous, as I trust the power that has created me (God), I know that everything I need for this life is taken care of. Remember, we always have the power to change our lives for the best. Follow your heart, allow it to lead you to your dreams. Ezekiel 36:26

Day 135

Yesterday, as I drove to pick up some tables I designed, two bald eagles flew twelve (12) feet above my car towards the drivers side. In my utter exhilaration, I rolled down the window to express my utter appreciation for them and to say God Bless You. The second bald eagle, flew a little lower, turned his/her head towards me and started to speak in the beauty of bald eagle's language. I was thrilled and in utter Awe from the entire experience. These majestic beings are so gorgeous as they soar across our skies, I, personally am exceedingly appreciative to have such beings on our planet. Majestic Beauty. 1 Chronicles 29:11

Day 136

Regardless of how many moons you have been on the planet, live your best life. Laugh often and much with yourself, friends, family, or your pets. Dance in the rain of life, decide to dance to your own beat, who cares if you have rhythm or not, as long as you are dancing. Dance in a corn field, dance down your country road, dance on your doorstep or front porch. Wherever you are...dance and decide to be happy for the mere fact that you can dance, moving your body as you wish. Dance in the ocean even. Just dance. Psalm 95:6

Day 137

I read recently that if we leave undisturbed in our hearts the things, circumstances we desire (meaning not to fret or worry over them) then each shall appear within their perfect time, space sequence. I love knowing this, it fills my heart with an immeasurable peace. Psalm 37:7

Day 138

Take a moment to stare at the formation of a cloud, as it lingers against the beautiful blue backdrop of the sky. Now take your thoughts to who created such beauty and be in Awe. Exodus 20:8-11

Day 139

Find a tree either in your yard or at a local park, or if you decide to travel to Yellow Stone, notice the groves in the tree trunk and the various shades of brown, or whether there are branches growing . Walk up to the tree and express your appreciation for it's existence, for the oxygen it creates for us to be able to breathe fresh air. Give the tree a hug and send the love to all of the trees all over the world, even to those that have not been planted yet. Psalm 23:6

Day 140

I recently checked out several books and DVD's from my local library on Dolphins and Humpback whales. Several years ago, while either dreaming or day dreaming, I saw an image of a Humpback whale swimming in the ocean looking at me with one eye. The image is ingrained in my heart and mind. In whatever manner you are able, (use paper bags, or bring your own cloth bag to the grocery store), use Eco friendly laundry detergent, visit one of the sites on save the Whales and Dolphins and practice living in a manner to assist in saving sea life as well as our planet. Matthew 21:22

Day 141

Well, a lot has changed since my last dialogue, I purchased a new computer since my laptop mouse froze and I was not able to access my writings. Today, as I took a lovely stroll around Lake Calhoun with a former colleague, in the midst of conversation, a total stranger walks past and says at the top of his voice, Gorgeous. What a lovely confirmation, I am now thanking our Creator for sending him along my path. Philippians 4:8

Day 142

Earlier in the day, on Day 140, I had an opportunity to wish a young lady a simply spectacular life on every level, explaining how the wish extends to every area of her life and lasts forever. Tears welled up in her eyes, as she placed her hand over her heart and said I feel completely blessed. I smiled and explained how this was my main intention. I truly believe this is one of the main reasons why I have shown up on the planet is to speak goodness into the life of others. Feel free to speak your goodness. Psalm 23:6

Day 143

As you read the words on the pages of this book, my wish is for you to have the same bliss and utter appreciation, knowing that I wish you the same Incredible Life on Every Level. My wishes always come true. Matthew 11:24-25

Day 144

Be comfortable with who you are...let yourself know every day how much you treasure yourself. If there are negative thoughts in your mind, remove them with Divine Love stating how they shall never return. Then, speak a positive affirmation to replace those thoughts. Allow this tapestry to be your new masterpiece for your Incredible Life. Ephesians 2:10

Day 145

Cherish yourself and those who are most precious to you...imagine your life with those special people evolving exactly as your hearts desires. See joy, happiness and unconditional love everywhere. Embrace this beautiful reality. Matthew 6:21

Day 146

Be patient with yourself, if you ate too many potato chips over the winter months and need to shed some pounds permanently, send you body unconditional love, seeing in your 'minds eye ' the healthy food and body you desire and live your life as though it already exists. Ephesians 6

Day 147

Be courageous and follow your dreams, make quiet time for day dreaming and envision your life exactly as your day dream. Decide to live knowing instinctively that every thing is unfolding naturally, Romans 8:28

Day 148

Possess an attitude of utter appreciation, gratefulness and gratitude for life. Be thankful for those souls who may show up to teach you how not to be. Be appreciative for those who you admire and if you wish, incorporate similar characteristics in your life that you have witnessed in those positive examples. You are a Masterpiece, painting the canvass of your life. 1 Thessalonians 5:16-18

Day 149

Today, I took time to visit with God, asking Him how the day was, whether or not God had anything on His mind He wished to talk about....I wished for a two way conversation and not just expressing everything on my heart. Amazingly, I finished the conversation feeling as though I had a chance to talk to my Best Friend, the Creator of the universe and in particular the Creator of you and me. James 1:19

Day 150

I realize that God does not need a thing, however, I still believe it is important to express my appreciation for every detail of my life. We are all on this journey and sometimes, we may feel challenged when we have a need to want to know every single detail of how our hearts desires shall unfold. This is the time to Trust. Let's know with certainty that our paths are illuminated and the perfect people, circumstances and situations shall appear at the perfect time. Breathe, relax and trust in the power that has created you. Colossians 3:15-17

Day 151

I am speaking to those of us that have been married before, be gentle with yourself. Know in your heart that you gave your marriage the best Year's ago, I sent my former husband God's Love,wishing him an excellent life on every level. I realize now that we were both too young to be married . Marriage is a precious union between two beautiful souls who love each other immensely. Be kind, respectful, communicate in a positive manner and decide to respect each other. These are a few solid pillars to build an incredible, precious, solid foundation on for one of the most important union of two souls. Matthew 11:28-30

Day 152

If we decide to live each day, loving and respecting each other, then 50 to 60 years later, we may look our husband in the eye (or wife) and share how much more in love we are today than years ago when our journey of love began. Embrace change and who you are, in each circumstance I believe this is an opportunity for us to grow as human beings on this precious planet called earth. Jeremiah 12:2

Day 153

I wish you utter happiness, bliss, joy and true love today and always. 1 Corinthians 13

Day 154

I wish you the courage to pursue your dreams and better yet, to visualize the dream into existence, living in a manner as though your life (the way you desire) already exists. 2 Peter 1:2

Day 155

Take time to nourish your body with healthy green veggies and food that is not genetically modified. Your body is a gift that stays with you during your entire lifetime. How exciting to know that based on what we choose to eat we have the opportunity to make our body very healthy. What an empowering, liberating truth. 1 Corinthians 6:19-20

Day 156

I love the sound of rain, beating against the house and nourishing the trees, grass and garden. I love the idea of purifying the air, which helps all living beings breathe better. What a gift the rain brings to us... Providing a free car wash and allowing each one of us to have a chance to 'dance in the rain' of life. Zechariah 10:1

Day 157

Over the years as I decided to 'dance in the rain ' of life, I am able to look back and realize that anything I thought was unsurmountable worked out perfectly, even better than I expected. Witnessing these occurrences first hand allows me to face today, tomorrow and the future knowing that life is completely fine and working out for my absolute best interests on every level. I know the same is true for you as well. Sit back and reflect upon your life, whatever area you wish to change, send it God's Love and prepare to witness the miracle of manifesting what you desire. Psalm 149:3

Day 158

Smile. Breathe deeply and just be today. Enjoy your own company. Become your own best friend. John 15:15

Day 159

Give a puppy a hug or a new home with you. Be in awe of the miracle of life. Write down what inspires you and view the words often. 2 Corinthians 4:16-18

Day 160

If or rather when you are faced with approaches or techniques that may differ from yours, kindly finish the assignment and decide not to take anything personally. Advice given to me by my favorite boss who convinced me nearly eight years ago to go into Professional Consulting. Proverbs 4:6-7

Day 161

Recently, I had to decide to walk away from a toxic friendship that I had for nearly 20 years. Initially, I felt guilty for walking away, however, when I did an inventory in my mind of how many times the conversations, events and circumstances were always about this person, I realized that my decision was correct and gave me back a life of peace, fun and spending time partaking in activities that I enjoy Conduct an inventory of your close relationships and decide to keep the ones that nourish your soul. Luke 19:10

Day 162

Experience utter bliss by sending the planet Divine Love from your heart, knowing that each place receiving this precious gift is being healed on spiritual levels that transcends to generations to come. Philippians 4:8

Day 163

Be kind to your parents, each one has done the best they knew how based on their own life experiences. Send your parents God's Love and thank our Creator in advance for meeting every one of their needs. Exodus 20:12

Day 164

Remember, we all have the answers to all of our lives questions inside our heart. Be still and listen to your heart. Remove any thoughts of fear, confusion and replace them with powerful thoughts of happiness, joy, bliss and envisioning your life with great health, wealth and overflowing with true love. Psalm 46:10

Day 165

Go outside and play in your garden today. If you do not have a garden yet, play on your deck, or walk around on the grass barefoot, whatever you do, take in the senses, breathe in the fresh air and bask in the beauty of the moment. Isaiah 61:3

Day 166

Witness the intelligence embedded in nature all around us. The trees know precisely which season is present. As I gaze out my window, I notice that the leaves on my trees are beginning to turn yellow. No one sent them a memo, neither did I go outside to announce to them that Fall is approaching. Be amazed at the wisdom that exists all around you, in every leaf, bug or animal. Proverbs 2:6

Day 167

Let your true love know how much you love them. Be sure to love and take very good care of yourself first before falling in love. So, when you do, your relationship is a healthy, happy and blissful one. Psalm 144:15

Day 168

Cherish the sunsets, the sunrises and the quietness in the still of the morning and evening dusk. Exodus 27:21

Day 169

Paint or draw a sunset today, or a flower or whatever catches your eye. Here is a picture of a sunset I captured from my window one evening. Enjoy. Psalm 113:3-5

Day 170

Surround yourself with positive, inspiring people and choose friends who are honest, ethical and who deeply respect you as a human being. Matthew 7:16

Day 171

Be completely pleased with your appearance, figure, and existence since you are the only <u>you</u> who has ever walked upon this planet. 2 Timothy 2:15

Day 172

Over this past weekend I had the lovely experience of attending a Print & Drawing event at the museum. I wished several precious souls an Incredible Life on every level, all who were very appreciative and wished me the same back. However, one precious soul, tilted her head back and laughed softly as she placed her hand over her heart. I was simply amazed and truly believe in the power of positive words. She thanked me profusely and then asked what makes me wish people this, I responded... to spread goodness all over the planet and invited her to do the same. Galatians 6:10

Day 173

To all my female cohorts...ladies, just when you think no one notices you...remind yourself that this is not true. I attended an Art Exhibit a few days ago where the artist gave a short introduction on his art. The entire time this gentleman spoke he made direct eye contact with me. Initially, I thought it was because he might have been nervous and needed a positive face to focus on. Later, however, after a tour and extended question and answer session, myself and other attendees asked if we may take a picture with him. To my amazement, he thanked me for all of my questions and comments and then proceeded to tell me how beautiful I am. I gracefully accepted his compliments and was amazed at how his language barrier was no longer an issue as he expressed his thoughts to me. Ladies, remember, we are beautiful exactly as we are and always noticed. 1 Peter 3:3-4

Day 174

Be kind, gentle and loving towards yourself in action and in your thoughts. Jude 1:20

Day 175

Have you taken a moment to realize just how spectacular you are today? You are literally an incredible work of art, a masterpiece, made perfectly and there is no one else like you on the planet. Cherish who you are. Genesis 1:27

Day 176

What are you doing at this very moment? Stop, take a moment to look at yourself in a mirror. Look into your eyes and tell yourself how pleased you are with who you are. Tell yourself that you have and continue to do a great job taking care of yourself and your family. Believe this with all of your heart and take a moment often to remind yourself of this truth. John 16:13

Day 177

For all of the precious single people (who are single by choice or not at the moment), look yourself in the eyes and remind yourself of how incredibly lovable and wonderful you are. Allow your heart to open to receive love from yourself and others. Enjoy the state of being single by choice and when the special someone comes along, you shall know who he/she is. Be confident, have fun in being yourself and believe that the special someone (he/she) shall show up at the perfect time and not a minute sooner. Psalm 25:5

Day 178

Treat yourself in your mind first and then manifest a very precious friend who is totally in your corner, who respects, appreciates and supports your views and friendship immensely. The beautiful aspect of day dreaming is that each of us has the innate power to manifest the circumstance or life we desire. Psalm 37 :3-4

Day 179

Use your power wisely and for the good of yourself and the planet. Proverbs 3:9-10

Day 180

Give yourself permission to live your own life. Decide not to be concerned about who approves or disapproves of your life. Your choices become your happiness. Joshua 24:15

Day 181

A precious family member recently married a women of his dreams and I am so happy for him. He looks fantastic 'standing in his own strength." Philippians 4:11-13

Day 182

Decide to 'stand in your own strength' in however way this looks for you. 2 Corinthians 12

Day 183

One of my treasured friends years ago always reminded me, whenever I may have been a little anxious, he always says,'You are fine, everything is alright.' His words have proven true over the years and whenever I am a little anxious I literally hear his voice even in my being, saying, 'You are fine, everything is alright, it shall all work out just fine.' What a treasure of a human being he is to myself and the planet. Proverbs 18:24

Day 184

Surround yourself with really neat people and if you view yourself as fortunate enough, select a few for long lasting friendships. Proverbs 22:11

Day 185

Be a good friend to yourself and then you are truly able to be a good friend to others. Ecclesiastes 49:10

Day 186

Plant a tree; plant some wild flowers and each season, marvel at the growth and the beauty of the creation. Psalm 1:3

Day 187

Most homes have dishwashers, several years ago while searching for a new home, I deliberately did not have a dishwasher installed and decided to wash my dishes by hand, granting me time to gaze out the window as I dry the dishes. This morning, as I washed the dishes, gazing out the window at the most beautiful day, I noticed a butterfly landing on one of the wildflowers I planted last season. The mere sight warmed my heart, since my overall intention was to attract more butterflies by planting all sorts of wildflowers. The benefits of planting wildflowers extend beyond lifetimes. Jeremiah 1:11-12

Day 188

As I am writing this message for today, I notice a man standing outside of the local library smoking a cigarette ...my wish for him and everyone else who may do the same, is to make a healthy decision to love yourself enough to stop. Marvel at and cherish the incredible body you live in. 1 Corinthians 3:16

Day 189

If you may be experiencing a not so happy moment or day, turn the tides and list people, places and things you are most appreciative of. Then, watch your moment or day turn around for the better.

Practice appreciating and being in Awe of life each day and any gloomy seconds, moments of days shall soon disappear. Matthew 24:35

Day 190

Wish the best for everyone and decide not to speak badly of anyone. As you live this way, endless goodness shows up in expected and unexpected ways. Matthew 24

Day 191

Believe in the power that created you. This power, whom I like to refer to as God can handle any circumstance or situation. There is no need for tears or worry, these are wasted emotions, since God has already worked out the details for your best interest. Philippians 2:13

Day 192

Breathe, breathe, breathe, focus on the positive and believe in the goodness of life and the kindness of a stranger. I have the honor of meeting kind people wherever I am, complete strangers on the plane, in line at the grocery store, or at the Orchestra or while traveling for vacation. Kindness extends everywhere. Galatians 6:9-10

Day 193

A few minutes ago, a bald eagle flew past the sun and cast a huge shadow on the tree outside my window. Regardless of where I may be in my home or in the yard, I always know that it is a bald eagle, which makes my soul soar. How amazing. Bask in whatever makes your soul soar. Isaiah 40:31

Day 194

Start believing in Angels, notice the so called coincidences. I personally believe we are assigned two Angels from birth which are assigned by God to illuminate our path along this precious journey called life. Luke 2:8-20

Day 195

Take a moment to thank God for your Angels.. Psalm 91:11-12

Day 196

After the next thunder storm, look for the Rainbow and make a positive wish. Write down the wish and review it later to confirm that it has comes true. Genesis 9:13-17

Day 197

Happiness is a state we all may participate in at any time. Psalm 121

Day 198

If you have a ton of clutter in your life make a decision to Simplify. As you Simplify, donating or selling clothing or items you have not used in six months to a year, your mind becomes clearer, thoughts are no longer cluttered. Clear away papers on your dining room table, on your dresser, wherever there may be clutter. Start reclaiming your clear thoughts and logical mind. Romans 8:38-39

Day 199

Who do you admire? I admire Julia Child. Read books on the person you admire and fill your soul with their noble attributes. In my mind, Julia was very humble as she invited Master Chefs into her home to share their recipes. I noticed while watching the episodes how most, if not all of her guest were truly honored to be in her presence and one could tell she felt the same way. Philippians 4:8

Day 200

If there is someone precious in your life that you need to make amends with, then make amends. However, if the relationship is truly over, wish the person well as you move onto the next chapter of your life in happiness. Proverbs 18:4

Day 201

Meditate, even for only 5 minutes to start. During this sacred time, clear your mind of any chatter, Focus on something you love, for instance a single red rose. Admire the beauty of the rose, the fragrance, the color. Taking the time to stop and be present for meditating relaxes your entire body and soul, allowing you to be more creative and free with your time and energy. Meditating opens the space to Attract only the best to you. Psalm 104

Day 202

Be kind to everyone you meet, kindness is a universal language and it starts with being kind at home. Psalm 103:17-22

Day 203

While attending events, truly visit with the people around you, listen more, talk less and be surprised at how much fun you are experiencing. Ecclesiastes 5:1-3

Day 204

It is very important in life to follow your own inner wisdom. One may listen to the advice of others...however ultimately, the final decision and direction one may take in life needs to be based on their own instinctive inner guidance. Proverbs 4:11

Day 205

Sit for 5 minutes each day (or longer if time permits) and meditate. Pay attention to your breath and clear your mind. Begin to envision the life you desire and already imagine yourself living that life. Psalm 33:6

Day 206

Each day during your time of meditating, or as you go along your day, offer up thoughts and/or prayers of gratitude to God for all of the goodness that shows up in your life and that has shown up over the years. Ephesians 5:20

Day 207

Send thoughts of God's Supreme Love to complete strangers as you walk past them in the grocery store, bus, plane, wherever you may be, send thoughts of healing love to penetrate their world, creating a beautiful planet of healthy, happy, healed souls. John 5:1-9

Day 208

Choose a life filled with Joy, Laughter and kind expressions. Hebrews 13

Day 209

Plant seeds of greatness in your conversations with others, fill your eyes and heart with compassion, communicating words sealed in kindness. 2 Chronicles 31:5

Day 210

Leave all lower frequencies and lower thoughts behind, fill your mind and heart with love, happiness, joy and respect for yourself and others. Nehemiah 8:10

Day 211

Release any thoughts of negativity that do not align with the life you desire to live. Psalm 23

Day 212

Give your dominant attention to joy, love, happiness and your heart's desires. Remove your attention off of what you do not want . Nehemiah 9 :5b

Day 213

Have faith that everything is working out for your highest good. All is perfect in your world. Matthew 5:48

Day 214

Transcend your knowing through your love, joy, thoughts and confidence in realizing everything in your world flows perfectly. Colossians 3:2

Day 215

Center your thoughts and realize as one of my favorite authors (Wayne Dyer) often quoted, 'You are a soul having a human experience'. Decide to simplify areas of your life that consume unnecessary time and energy. Joshua 1

Day 216

As you walk forth in faith in the power that has created you, deciding not to clutter your thoughts with uncertainty; You shall start to notice all of the desires of your heart unfolding in perfect synchronicity. Jeremiah 29:11-14

Day 217

Cherish each Season of Life and those who mean the world to you. Ecclesiastes 3:1-8

Day 218

Rid your vocabulary and mind of the phrase, "it is what it is". Each one of us has the power of our mind and thoughts to create a life that suits us perfectly. Decide not to give your power away. Hebrews 4:12-13

Day 219

Mediate on, 'my life is improving every day, everything I need comes to me easily and effortlessly, granting me my heart's desires.' Psalm 119:105

Day 220

Express your heart, I often say, thank you God for granting me this incredible beautiful day. Thank you for the wild flowers that know when to grow at the perfect time....thank you for the beautiful colors of pink, fuschia, yellows and variations of purples. Thank you for the sweet smell of wild roses. Luke 11:28

Day 221

All of life is a roadmap of experiences that has led us to the point where we are today. Choose positive choices and circumstances with a heart filled with gratitude. Express appreciation by continuing to live a life that causes your soul to soar. Psalm 18:30

Day 222

I am heading on a really wonderful trip in two days. I am so excited to visit this place, I know similar to everywhere I go, whether in my neighborhood or traveling within the US and abroad, wonderful people are everywhere. Matthew 7:24

Day 223

Let go and trust. Trust the process of positive living. If ever you find your thoughts wondering, direct them back to the deep knowing that everything is working out for your highest good, as one of my favorite authors (Louise Hay) says. 'Out of this and all situations, only good shall come'. Matthew 4:4

Day 224

Quite honestly, I feel so much better and lighter as I focus my thoughts on positive affirmations I have created for myself. Such as, I am loved and I am lovable, the perfect romantic relationship has shown up in my life at the perfect time. I am so appreciative of him and he is of me. Focus on what brings you calm. Matthew 8:23-27

Day 225

Create a list of positive affirmations that is tailor made for your life Even, at first, you may not believe the affirmation 100 %, decide to repeat them each day and you shall notice your energy shifting to a more healthy place. 2 Timothy 1:7

Day 226

Decide to rid your mind of gossip or associating with others who live at that lower energy level.

You may instead, change the conversations to something general, such as the weather or if the person is into gardening. Focus on the positive. Otherwise, the negativity will drag you down. James 1:19

Day 227

Lately, I have decided to go inward and spend time basking in the knowledge that my soul possess. Each one of us has a deposit of the infinite wisdom inside of us. Tap in through spending time in quietness and be guided by this incredible source of light. Matthew 5:14-16

Day 228

Joy, infuse your life with joy. Wake up each morning prior to stepping out of bed, or viewing your email or cell phone messages and speak it aloud, "I am choosing joy in all of my interactions today." Notice how joy show up as if magically. Zephaniah 3:17

Day 229

Focus on peacefulness. Choose peaceful thoughts, decide on kindness instead of wanting to express you were right. Hebrews 12:2

Day 230

Change yourself instead of attempting to change others. Be the person you wish others to be and you shall start to notice those positive people showing up in your life. Psalm 30:5

Day 231

Live your adventure and resign from the population of those who live 'lives of quiet desperation.' John 10:10

Day 232

Each day I receive a positive quote on my phone, I love the one for today and wished to share it with the world. "I open my heart and allow wonderful things to flow into my life." What an incredibly beautiful quote. Enjoy! Psalm 27:19

Day 233

Allow life to come to you. Eliminate chasing after people, circumstances or events. I have discovered that if you are meant to attend a concert, a play or work with a certain company, everything in life aligns for the circumstances to occur. Serendipity and happenstance become friends. 1 Corinthians 16:14

Day 234

Even though the leaves are turning and gently flowing to the ground, almost as if partaking in a ritual dance or passage, there on the tree branch sits a beautiful golden finch and a chickadee basking in the warmth and sacredness of the morning sun. John 8:36

Day 235

Infuse your entire day with positivity. Change any thought to a positive one. 1 Corinthians 2:6-16

Day 236

What a joy to discover the power each of us has to change our lives for the better. Affirm goodness for yourself and those you love. 1 Corinthians 4:1

Day 237

A few minutes ago a ton, (at least 500 birds or more) flew to the trees in my yard. I wish I could record the sound, each song was incredibly beautiful. Look for your adventure, find your 'bird convention today'. Psalm 96

Day 238

Whatever you wish to change in your life, approach the journey with a heart filled with love. Take care of yourself first, by expressing to yourself how treasured, precious and loved you truly are, by yourself and by your Creator. Spend five (5) or more minutes a day filling up your soul with positive thoughts and then you shall find more time and energy to spend time with those you cherish or are beginning to cherish. Proverbs 4:8

Day 239

Be happy wherever you are. Whether at home, traveling to a fun place or walking your pet around the lake or on the beach. Romans 15:3

Day 240

Today, have you planned anything truly exciting for you to do? If not, decide on a short trip to Cape Cod, or a fun place where you live, have a movie night with some close friends or your special someone. Do something to add more joy into your life today. 1 Chronicles 16:26-27

Day 241

A year or so ago, I kept repeating an affirmation for wonderful new friends to be added to my life. I eliminated friends that were no longer pleasant to spend time with. Today, I have several new friends who are fun, positive and a joy to be around. John 15:13

Day 242

Give yourself a vacation from a situation, person or circumstance that may involve drama. Then, as you visit with the person, place or circumstance again and notice that nothing has changed, choose the healthy road and either reduce the time spent or no longer associate with the person, place or conditions. Luke 15:7

Day 243

As I thought about which words (or the method of expressing these words) to the precious souls reading my books....I decided to devote the next few days to positive affirmations I have done over the years to create the life I now have today. My affirmations may be useful to your life, or provide a starting point for you to create affirmations specific to your life. Either way, my wish is for everyone to be inspired, as you create goodness for yourself. Namaste. Jude 1:2

Day 244

Existing Home: Thank you home for all of the wonderful memories I have had here, for keeping me warm and surrounded by beauty, for the memories of my family, friends and love ones being entertained and sharing lovely meals within these walls. I now send you away in love to a new owner, who shall love and cherish you as I have these past 12 years. John 14:1

Day 245

Sale of Existing Home: The perfect person interested in purchasing my home shall make an offer in cash for the exact amount that I am selling my home for. The closing (including the processing of all the necessary paperwork and documents) and interaction will be fun and easy with no contingencies. 3 John:1-4

Day 246

New Home: I am living in a beautiful new home with lots of bald eagles flying by, Bald eagles have made a nest on my property. I have wonderful new neighbors who are some of the nicest people in the world and I live in a safe, beautiful and peaceful environment. I have purchased my dream home at a price I may easily afford. Galatians 5:22-23

Day 247

New Home (continued): I have my own well, eliminating any water bills. I own my own propane tank, eliminating any service fees for renting a tank and as a result, my propane is purchased at a discount since I own my own tank. I am able to purchase the propane at a discount with the pre-buy program, reducing my electricity costs and living an eco-friendly life on all levels. Psalm 121:7-8

Day 248

New Home (continued): I have space for a lovely garden where I am able to grow fresh vegetables, strawberries, black raspberries, honey berries and elderberries. I am experiencing an abundant harvest enabling me to share generously of the produce from my wonderful garden with both friends and strangers. The organically grown produce is delicious and healthy for my body and provides the perfect nutrients for my well being and others. Colossians 3:23-24

Day 249

Car: You may create an affirmation that works specifically for you. The affirmation I am listing is from a few years ago when I was searching for a new car. I hardly ever work with car dealerships, however, I met the best sales person ever and purchased my Honda Fit from him. My affirmation was 'the perfect new car is awaiting me to purchase it. The perfect color, price and build exists in my new car. I am purchasing an extremely reliable car from a trustworthy sales person at a price I may easily afford. I am receiving excellent gas mileage on the car as well. I love and cherish my new car. Life is fantastic'. Philippians 4:4-8

Day 250

Career: I am working in the perfect environment in a career I admire, working with professional, fun filled individuals, who are honest and ethical. I work with people who love and respect me and who I love and respect. My engagements are fun and easy for me and I am paid very nicely. Deuteronomy 8

Day 251

Old Business: I am thankful for all of the clients I have had and worked for through the various consulting firms. Thank you contacts at these consulting firm for keeping me gainfully employed. I thank and also forgive those of you who have offered me rates lower than what I requested and others who have never seem to have an assignment for me. I am sending each circumstance and consulting firm along with the contact away and out of my life forever in Love, never to return. (with the exception of my two long term clients I have had for a total of 7 and 8 years). I am eternally grateful for the income I received for working on various assignments through these consulting firms and for some of the precious clients I have met. Now, it is time for me to move onto new *opportunities and work for myself, representing myself to my own excellent clients. I am thrilled to have this new opportunity to open my heart, mind and soul to receive my new clients. I open my arms wide to receive these blessings now and forevermore. Thank you God. Proverbs 10:22*

Day 252

Own Business: I am gainfully self-employed working with wonderful new clients who love and respect me and I love and respect them. I am working with honest, ethical people, in lovely locations who require my assistance on various engagements that are fun and easy for me. I am also working two consecutive months or more as an Inspirational Speaker, holding Workshops, Seminars, Conferences and Retreats around the world. I am gainfully self-employed as I self publish my books and lovely souls are attending my sessions, purchasing my books, ebooks, CD's and DVD's and attending my speaking engagements in droves . I am making a ton of money and I am comfortable with it. Clients find me and I am truly delighted to have an opportunity to finally live my Life's purpose and to be paid handsomely for doing so. The perfect people show up for my Inspirational Speaking engagements and I am honored to share the wisdom of creating their desired life with each one of them. Ecclesiastes 5:19

Day 253

Romantic Relationship: I am loved and lovable and deserve an incredible romantic relationship. Ephesians 5:22-33

Day 254

Romance: I am worthy of love. True love comes to me, I do not need to chase after it. The perfect romantic relationship finds me. My partner loves and respects me and I love and respect him. We live together wonderfully and enjoy spending time in the garden, hiking, biking, traveling and cooking together and sharing truths from the Word of God with others. Life is truly good to both of us and we love, respect and honor each other. 2 Timothy 3:16-17

Day 255

One of my favorite authors, 'Louise Hay' says this quote and I have read it in her books or listened to it on one of her many CD's, Tbe name of the DVD is 'You Can Heal Your Life". "Life loves me, life loves me. Everything is working out for my highest good. Out of this situation only good shall come and I am safe." I use this quote for any and all areas of my life that I wish to improve for the best. Psalm 31:3

Day 256

Abundance: My income is always increasing, I am working in my chosen career and making a very good living, I am thankful for the abundance that Life continues to offer me and everyone else. John 6:35

Day 257

The perfect answers shall come to me about this (name the situation or circumstance). I often do this whenever I have to make a decision on whether or not to accept an invitation to a social event, concert, or job offer. I allow myself a day or two to sleep on the decision and then make the decision based on a stance of strength and not through being reactive. Remember, at all times we have the power and the grace to live our lives based on our true heart's desire. James 3:13

Day 258

Another favorite quote from a tea bag I see often is, "Act, do not react". Acts 10

Day 259

I believe Life is simply fantastic on every level and there is goodness to witness and bask in wherever we may go. Psalm 97:11-12

Day 260

Smile, it is contagious. Smiling warms your heart and the recipients and before you know it, a warm smile has been sent around the world. Psalm 96:1-2

Day 261

Another firm thing I believe is that Kindness is a universal language. Even if you do not speak the same language, people may see the kindness expressed in your eyes, which is the window to the soul. Spread seeds of kindness wherever you are and reap the benefits of a beautiful life. Psalm 98:1-2

Day 262

Say to yourself, yes, I can do this. I am smart, I am intelligent, I am knowledgable and exceedingly wise. All of the answers I need for this situation have been revealed to me and I am completely successful. Thank you Life. Psalm 97:1

Day 263

Hug yourself. Tell yourself how special you are and hug yourself. Look at your body and send God's Love to every single limb, area and to your heart. Psalm 100:1-2

Day 264

Each day, nourish your soul with a beautiful day dream of living the life you desire. Before you realize it, you shall experience living this kind of life on a continuous basis. Proverbs 10:3-4

Day 265

Only people who are interested in my absolute well being come into my life and all others are sent away in love, never to return. Proverbs 24:1-2

Day 266

I am sending love to all of the trees, shrubs and bushes in my yard and around the world. I am so thankful for the oxygen these trees produce, enabling myself and the rest of the world to benefit from the clean, crisp healthy air. Ezekiel 17:24

Day 267

I am so grateful for the opportunity to recycle and help save our beautiful planet. Psalm 24:1

Day 268

I am so appreciative of all the sea life and the intelligence of Dolphins and Humpback Whales. I am so fortunate as well as the rest of the world to have these sea animals on our planet. Psalm 24:2

Day 269

I am so thankful for nature and all of the precious animals. Birds show me how to live peacefully, even in the most intense winters birds find food in the fields, off of the grass which has turned to seed for them to feast upon. Just as the birds are always provided for (Matthew 6:25-34) so are we.

Day 270

Here is sending you an enormous hug. You deserve it. Blessings on your soul. Psalm 103:1

Day 271

Expect Miracles every day and take time to give thanks for each one showing up at the exact and precise time in your life. Trusting completely in God's timing that this is the moment it is supposed to present itself to you. Exodus 23:20

Day 272

Choose to see the beauty in life....be grateful for all that you are and for actually showing up on the planet!!!!! Send immense Love to those you cherish and to complete strangers who need the encouragement. Psalm 25:4-5

Day 273

Cherish the moments you have with your parents, since one day, you shall have the opportunity to live on your own, have your own life and may not have as much time to visit with them as you do now. Psalm 17

Day 274

Cherish all friendships and relationships that are truly important to you. Share your heart with them, true friends and relationships are safe to share your deepest dreams with. If you should discover otherwise, then choose wisely what to share. Ask yourself if this friendship meets your definition of what a true friend really is to you. Proverbs 18:24

Day 275

Give yourself permission to say, no thank you to an event, a request or anything you have not decided to participate in, even if it is at the last minute. Be true to yourself. Nine times out of ten, if you waited until the last minute, on a subconscious level you may have not really been interested in the event. Instead, you are just filling up empty time and space. Decide to use your time wisely and in meaningful ways. Ecclesiastes 3:1-8

Day 276

Spread kindness through a smile, a kind gesture, a kind word. Similar to breathing in fresh clean air every day to clear your mind, heart and soul, spread kindness. In doing so, you are relieving your soul and the world of all toxic thoughts. Genesis 2:7

Day 277

Bask in the beauty of who you are, spend time doing what you love instead of attempting to change friends, family or loved ones into what you would like them to be. Believe me, the person most suited for you shall appear when you are off having a simply fabulous time with your life. Psalm 104:1-35

Day 278

Enjoy the company of the person sitting next to you on a plane, bus, or train. There are incredibly lovely people everywhere. James 1:27

Day 279

Share your heart and soul with the one you love. See the good in them and good shall increase everywhere. Loose yourself in a deep kiss. Psalm 85:10

Day 280

Patience, kindness and integrity are incredible garlands to grace your heart, soul and life with forever. Galatians 6:9

Day 281

I personally love witnessing the inexpressible joy on teenagers, adults and people of all races, colors and creeds, when I wish them a completely Incredible Life on Every level. This past Sunday, a young teenager girl,tears welling up in her eyes, initially reached out to give me a huge hug and then placed her hand over her heart and said thank you. I am truly honored to wish such an incredible wish on everyones lives. I am truly blessed just by the experience, Spread the goodness, everywhere and pray complete and utter goodness for the lives of our teenagers and their families. Mark 11:22-25

Day 282

Create a budget for the fun of it. List some line items you wish to set funds aside for and watch in utter amazement at how the rest of your life is fine-tuned. Proverbs 16:3

Day 283

Walk outside and as the snow falls gently to the earth, dance with a snowflake. Jeremiah 31:13

Day 284

Plant a tree every year to assist in the preservation of the planet and the replenishment of Christmas trees, logging or other activities that utilize our forests. Psalm 50:10

Day 285

As the universe sends you treasured friends, bask in the happiness of those friendships because each one is a true treasure. Matthew 6:19-21

Day 286

Decide to have the faith and courage to live your dream, start your own business and be excellent at it. Speak positive words into your soul each day, believing with all of your heart that there is enough supply for everyone on the planet. Say to yourself, the perfect people who are in need of my product, services workshops, etc, find me. Then, send up a silent prayer of gratitude for the true abundance. Hebrews 11:1

Day 287

Pay attention to someone who is constantly wanting to befriend you. If you decide to spend time with the person and each encounter is filled with drama, decide to silently send them away and out of your life in love. Recently, an acquaintance called to invite me to a play and I knew instinctively that the person only wanted me to pay for the ticket she was now 'stuck' with. Our instincts let us know immediately who is a true friend. Follow your intuition. Job 38:36-38

Day 288

Open your arms each day and say an affirmation of how you deserve the best in every area of your life and that you accept the best now. Thank our Creator for the opportunity to have this abundance, happiness and endless joy and prosperity. Proverbs 11:25

Day 289

I am now working for myself and I love it. I have wonderful new clients who I love working with and who love working with me. My clients love my work product so much that I am hired for even more engagements. I am gainfully self-employed and making very good money and very comfortable and grateful for being gainfully self-employed. Proverbs 19:8

Day 290

Believe in yourself, be your biggest fan, loudest cheerleader. Step back and pay attention to how Life rises up to meet you with everything that you need to live your Life's most sacred dreams. Deuteronomy 5:33

Day 291

Hug your bed in the morning and say thank you to the comfortable sheets, pillows and bed frame for granting you a very restful nights sleep. Psalm 4:8

Day 292

Thank the appliances in your kitchen for keeping your food fresh, or heating up your water for tea in the morning, be appreciative of everything in your life. Psalm 107:9

Day 293

List 10 things each day you are grateful for...stop and take in a deep breath before you think of complaining and replace it with a grateful thought and a kind word. Proverbs 15:1

Day 294

Rid your conversations of gossip and speaking badly about others. Replace those thoughts with how you intend to live your life for the best and become a person who contributes positively to the planet. Believe in the Power of who created you (God). Live the dream, write the book, write the screen play, design the most elegant clothing line, or become the interior decorator you have dreamed to be. Be the best engineer, scientist, pilot, baker, chef, mechanic...whatever you choose to be. Isaiah 28:29

Day 295

Parents, let your young adults go, you have done a fine job 'raising them'. Now, once the children have grown up, allow them to live their own lives. Each child is now an adult and has all of the attributes embedded within their being to Soar. Parents, decide to become their friends now, it is okay...trusting that all of the things you have taught them along your beautiful journey together has become the compass which illuminates their path. Proverbs 22:6

Day 296

In-laws, accept the person your offspring decides to date, befriend or marry without judgement, extend love to that person and accept them into your life as family because you trust the heart of your offspring to live an incredible life as he/she has witnessed you living. Romans 15:7

Day 297

Brother or sister-in-laws, be the positive part of the equation as your sibling accepts a new mate, work on loving yourself first so you may love others for who they are. John 13:20

Day 298

Each one of us is our own hero, our perfect caretaker of our souls. Colossians 1:15-20

Day 299

Be true to each day, decide to exercise, drink plenty of water in an act of thanking your beautiful body for allowing your soul to live there comfortably each day. Psalm 118:24

Day 300

Quite honestly, it feels Awesome to reach Day 300 as I am writing this 365 day book to encourage souls all over the world! Smile, play hop scotch with a good friend, even if you are past 20. Recently, I retaught myself how to knit. I completely love it and have since knit several baby blankets and prayer blankets blessing little ones and friends with scripture verses from the bible. Knit a tapestry of kindness, joy and love into your life. Psalm 139

Day 301

Follow your heart, your higher self knows the way and leads you down a path specially tailor-made for you.... your very own 'Red Carpet'. Psalm 23

Day 302

Forgive from the heart, love family members unconditionally, realize their attitude, actions and disposition on life may never change or match your beliefs, which is fine. You have so much to be appreciative of and have the power to set healthy boundaries to truly be the person you either desire to be or have become. Psalm 9:1

Day 303

If you have the opportunity and are still in contact with your high school sweet heart, tell him or her how much you appreciate them, thank them for all of those special memories of years long ago. Psalm 8:1

Day 304

"History" is a version of the person, people or collective body expressing their perspective. The account may not be all inclusive of all people, races and creeds and their contributions made during that particular time of

history. Decide to make your own history, be sure to fill it with kindness, happiness, love, consideration and respect for all living beings. Psalm 37:1-4

Day 305

Today, as I ventured outside, on another new journey to a warehouse/fabric store, I met so many wonderful people, wishing each an Incredible Life on Every level. Two people, independent of each other asked the same question, "Why or what has made me wish people such a beautiful wish". I explained that I truly desire to spread goodness all over the planet and decided to start wishing folks this 7 years ago, instead of wishing someone a good day, week or year, I thought, wishing them an excellent eternity covers it all. John17:3

Day 306

Follow the dreams of your heart. Rid yourself of Ego, fear or any other lower energies. See beyond yourself and picture how powerful your positive message or action is to the world. John 14:6

Day 307

Stand in the beauty of who you are. Stand in your gentle and quiet strength. Life is most certainly beautiful on every level. John 6:25-59

Day 308

Each one of us showed up on this planet for a reason, for a purpose, explore the road, enjoy the journey and most importantly believe in the Power that has created you, (which I personally, like to refer to as God). This power has made each one of us perfectly with our own tailored made dreams, follow those dreams and live your bliss. Psalm 20:4

Day 309

Take a moment and look at the shape, color and smell the fragrance of your favorite flower. Home grown Roses are my favorite. The aroma is exquisite, no one has ever mastered the aroma in a perfume, only God has the blueprint. 1 Chronicles 28

Day 310

What do you love to do? What have you always wished to do. For me, I have always wanted to draw and paint. One day, I took out my sketch pad and drew the flowers that are on my late grandmothers beautiful handkerchief. The feeling of serenity flooded my senses as I took my time and drew this pattern, I encourage you to carve out time, even if for a half hour to do something or start something you have always wanted to do. Remove all time pressures and constraints. Each week, or every other day or once a month make an appointment with yourself to bask in this time of creating/doing what your heart has desired to do for so long. Psalm 37:4

Day 311

I know there is another book inside of me to write because I have this incredible feeling of excitement knowing that day 365 shall arrive soon and yet, I have so much to share, so much to say to all of my beautiful readers. Each one of you are jewels within yourself. Thank you for showing up and finding my words very useful for your life, happiness and purpose. Proverbs 8:11

Day 312

Bask, bask, bask in the knowledge of who you are. Know for certain that at all times, you have the answer to your question. Yes, you have the solution to the puzzle or situation. Go within and the answers, solutions and happiness shall appear. Proverbs 3:15-18

Day 313

One of my favorite authors is Doreen Virtue, she has and continues to write many amazing books, one of her books named 'Angel Numbers' is one of my favorite. Lately, while driving, I noticed 313....I am going to quote what it says here. "Lean upon the positive and loving energies of the ascended masters who surround you right now, as they're lifting your thoughts to higher levels of happy living." Thank you so very much Doreen Virtue for all of the incredible goodness you spread all over the planet. We all love you very, very much. Proverbs 3:5-6

Day 314

Read books from people you truly admire, then be inspired to write your own. Mark 10:27

Day 315

If there is someone you love and respect for example, I love old reruns of Julia Child opening her home to upcoming or already renown chefs. I love watching her interaction with each one and the incredible humility of her working with each one to include the chef's recipe in her repertoire. Julia's grace and utter excitement for life is absolutely contagious. Colossians 3:12

Day 316

I also love witnessing how in 'Awe' the chef's are to be in Julia's presence and cook in her kitchen. Both experiences are true treasures for me to witness. Find someone or something that is a true treasure to you and enjoy each moment of basking in witnessing the goodness. One year for my birthday, I traveled to the

Smithsonian to see her kitchen on display and stayed there for hours, imagining in my mind what it might have been like to cook in her kitchen with her. Simply Amazing. Proverbs 22:4

Day 317

This message is particularly for anyone wishing to write a book. Please, follow your instincts and all of the signs that appear along your path to write and publish your book. There are billions of lovely souls on the planet, trust that the perfect person and audience shall purchase your books and be completely inspired and encouraged by your words. Jeremiah 17:7-8

Day 318

Stand aside and allow the universe to fill you with the words in which to write. Throw away fear as if like a worn out garment that no longer serves you. Psalm 102:26-28

Day 319

Ralph Waldo Emerson and Henry David Thoreau are two of my favorite authors. I love their perspective on life. I love the friendship they had with each other. I love the message of simplifying my life on every level. Matthew 6:19-21

Day 320

Thoreau is correct, there is a subtleness in nature, a peaceful assurance of every thing unfolding perfectly, in it's perfect time. Numbers 6:24-26

Day 321

It is important to believe in ourselves, to believe in our dreams and to be confident of the strength we have inside to share those dreams with the world. Hebrews 10:35-36

Day 322

Even in writing, my soul wishes to cherish each one of these messages for the day. Slow down, breathe, bask in the goodness of this moment. Know that this is the one moment I am writing a positive message to you the reader on Day 322. Do something fun today, by yourself or with a friend or someone truly special to you. Attend your favorite play, or movie, go for a walk along the beach or lake, enjoy the time, life is truly a gift. James 1:17

Day 323

Earlier today in the fabric store, I met a lovely couple who I had the opportunity to wish an Incredible Life on every level. The lady showed myself and several other patrons the 7 quilts she made for her siblings for this upcoming Christmas Holiday. The quilts were breathtakingly beautiful, each one had a piece of their mothers wedding dress and some of the brides maids dresses in the design. As I spoke with her, she shared how she grew up on a farm and intends to sew copies of their old barn on the back of the quilt with a copy of their Dad's favorite scarf and present the quilts to family members, including her parents for Christmas. How priceless. My soul is richer from the encounter with this precious soul. Jeremiah 29:11-14

Day 324

One of the male helpers in the fabric store came over to view the quilts. Immediately, he asked the woman if she was sentimental and if he could take her out on a date. I looked over at the ladies husband, who stood there smiling, not saying a word and watched as she explained that she was married. The male helper attempted to convince me that 'fooling around' was fun. I stood in my strength and said, no, I do not believe in 'fooling around', I believe in true love, faithfulness and being in complete and utter love with each other. Stand in your strength today and dismiss anyone gently (in your heart with love) who attempts to convince you to follow their splintered values. 1 Peter 4:8

Day 325

The nice lady with the quilts leaned over to me and said, I believe in true love as well. She married her high school sweetheart. Give yourself permission to believe in true love, decide to give yourself the best in every area of your life. Never settle. I recently witnessed someone special staring at me with eyes filled with true love. I am placing the situation in God's hands to see how everything unfolds. I had recently traveled back from Boston and this precious soul prayed for my safe return. Song of Songs 8:6

Day 326

Two years ago, I had a few dresses made for myself. After realizing the price the person charged I decided that I may easily teach myself how to sew again. Today, I purchased three fabrics for three different dresses which are all 100% cotton for less than the cost of one dress the person charged me two years ago. We may at any time decide to take our power back and teach ourselves how to sew, skate, ski, knit or whatever catches your fancy. Exodus 35:25-35

Day 327

If you find that a group, organization or charity you may have been giving to or spending time with no longer works for where you are in your life, send the people, place and establishment love and clear your schedule to allow something even more wonderful, more in line with who you are presently to appear. Matthew 5:13

Day 328

Look into a new adventure such as gardening, going hiking in your favorite park, visiting a new place in your area that you did not know existed. The change of scenery may be amazing. Malachai 3:6

Day 329

If, by chance, you feel inclined to want to wish people an incredible life on every level, however, you are shy; what I did in the beginning was wish them this in my heart. I fly often and I would say a silent wish for a Wonderful Life on every level, or an Incredible Life on every level, in my heart to the entire plane. Hebrews 13:8

Day 330

Today, I literally love seeing the utter expression of gratitude, joy and heart felt thanks on each persons face as I wish them this incredible wish of A Spectacular Life on every level. For me, it is the perfect wish and I explain how the wish extends to every nook and cranny of their lives and how it only gets better and better and the only thing they need to do is take it in like beautiful rays of sunshine or like a breath of fresh air. Deuteronomy 31:8

Day 331

Planting and spreading seeds of goodness all over the planet shall most definitely reap a life of new and existing 'treasured friends'. Each one of our words are powerful, speak goodness into your lives and everyone around you...and especially to those you love and cherish. Isaiah 49:16

Day 332

Remember, You are Perfect exactly as you are. God only creates Masterpieces. Isaiah 40:11

Day 333

I believe many people are Angels in disguise. Recently, I flew in to surprise my Mom at a nursing home she lived at temporarily. As I visited for a week, one of her nurses (all of which I believe are Angels) came in one day and as she served my Mom, asked who I and my brother were. My Mom explained that we are her daughter and son. This lovely nurse named Vitaline Alexandre said something so beautiful, so poetic, that I decided to mention it here in my book. "Your daughter is beautiful! You took time to draw her beautifully." Wow! I love Vitaline's expression, if we truly think about it, we are 'drawing' our lives, each day that we live. Draw beautifully!!! John 8:1-11

Day 334

Embrace the goodness and beauty all around you. I most certainly did the day Vitaline Alexandre said these most powerful and beautiful words to my Mom. Isaiah 33:17

Day 335

Earlier today, I listened to an author named Kris Carr on Hay House Radio. I agree with her suggestion to reward ourselves when we have accomplished something, instead of rushing off to the next 'to do list'. Isaiah 28:5

Day 336

Today, I am devoting myself to eating healthy and eliminating foods that are filled with ingredients that cause inflammation in my body and joints. (e.g. potato starch, tapioca starch, rice flour, wheat, xanthum gum, rice starch, carrageen, any sort of gums or colorings). Our bodies deserve clean foods to provide these wonderful Masterpieces, which I like to refer to as ourselves to thrive. Psalm 27:4

Day 337

Remember, the fewer the ingredients, the better the product. Take one meal a week and create it from scratch, all natural ingredients. Eat more veggies, start a small garden and eat the bounty of the goodness from the earth. Psalm 29:2

Day 338

Meditate on the dancing movement of one snowflake or several and give thanks in your heart for their creation, each snowflake is uniquely it's own design. Romans 1:20

Day 339

Start drawing, painting, skiing, attending or holding seminars on what you love. Give yourself permission to live in happiness and utter bliss. Isaiah 52:7

Day 340

Take baths, use bath crystals and scents that allow you to sleep soundly, naturally and are excellent for your body. 1 Corinthians 6:19-20

Day 341

Pamper yourself either at home or at a day SPA. If you are single, schedule regular massages either monthly or quarterly. If coupled, schedule your own special SPA day with your special someone and bask in the beauty of each other. Psalm 96:9

Day 342

What is Sacred to you? Spend time honoring the sacredness in your life. Exodus 3:5

Day 343

Believe in Miracles, each one occurs every single day, all day long. Acts 3:16

Day 344

Each one of us is so worthy, so blessed, so cared for. What incredibly powerful words to live by. Believe this is true for you. 1 Timothy 4:14

Day 345

Babies are excellent examples for all of us to learn from. Each one lives in utter bliss in the comfort of their Mommy and Daddy's arms. Never, have we ever seen a baby express concerns of where their meal shall come from, or what clothes to wear, or what have you. Each one is completely content in their parents arms, even if all they had to wear was a diaper. Let's have the same trust with our souls with God. Matthew 6:25-34

Day 346

Each one of us has a Creator, which I like to refer to as God, who takes care of all of our desires intrinsically. Believe with complete certainty that all of what you may need is already provided to you. (the new job, new client, new true love relationship, location to hold a Workshop and people arriving who are drawn to hear the words you wish to share with them). 1 Corinthians 12:31

Day 347

You are more powerful than you realize. Imagine, day dream, envision the life you desire and start living as though this already exists. Be prepared to be utterly amazed. Habakkuk 1:5

Day 348

Cherish, cherish, cherish, laugh, laugh, laugh, smile, smile, smile. Dance, dance, dance. Have fun and listen to your heart, it contains the blueprint to your soul. Ephesians 2:10

Day 349

Imagine a group of people, reliable friends who you may rely upon for exchanging great ideas, who may be your true confidants and watch how the universe orchestrates the occurrence of these wonderful souls. Acts 17:26

Day 350

Start a new adventure. (sewing a dress, knitting a hat, visiting a town you have never been to). Life is most certainly worth living and changing your thoughts to positive ones illuminates a beautiful path before you to discover each and every moment. Go for it, Change those thoughts to positive ones and start truly living! Proverbs 3:1-4

Day 351

Each day, practice saying positive thoughts/words to yourself. Continue this practice indefinitely and watch how your soul believes these great words and starts to blossom as a result of it. Colossians 3:1-2

Day 352

Remember to say thank you for any kindness received, compliment, kind gesture and send the person Divine Love, either verbally or in your heart. Philippians 2:1-2

Day 353

What is truly exciting to me is that each day, every moment of my life, I may send powerfully positive prayers to each and every soul on the planet. Each and every day, I may wish a total stranger a completely Incredible Life on Every level and witness, first hand, how those powerful words change the persons life for eternity. Each persons eyes light up and I have the honor of witnessing their expression of inexpressible joy, as though their soul soaks in the goodness. Beautiful, simply beautiful. 1 Thessalonians 5:16-19

Day 354

Walk and live gently on this beautiful planet. Send immense love to the ocean and all of those lovely sea animals, (Humpback whales, Bottlenose dolphins) there is an amazement of sea life all over the planet. Genesis 13:17

Day 355

Public Speaking: As you decide to become a public speaker, look at your audience of precious souls who traveled to the Workshop, Conference or Seminar to hear exactly what you wish to share. Believe your positive words make all the difference in their lives. Infuse beauty, God's Holy Spirit, goodness and the truth of the power that lies within each of us. Leave any hesitation or uncertainty at the door. 2 Corinthians 3:17

Day 356

Truly, our messages whether written down in books, or on powerpoint presentations, DVD recordings or CD's is all about the message we have for those precious souls who show up to listen to our words. Be sure to believe in your words of great encouragement since your intention is to encourage their souls and thus, enable them to change their lives for the best. John 14:16

Day 357

Viewing our Divine Purpose in this light, this truth, allows us to remove the focus from ourselves and say, How may I serve? (as one of my favorite authors, Dr. Wayne Dyer has said on countless occasions). Speaking then becomes easy, natural and we focus on how our words may be conduits and a healing salve for the hearts of so many precious souls. Malachi 3:17-18

Day 358

Kindness is a universal language. Decide to be an example of kindness to the world. John 14:26

Day 359

Rid your soul, mind and being of gossip, speak only good of others and watch your life and the world be infused with goodness and blossom beautifully. Isaiah 40:8

Day 360

Be yourself and someone's 'biggest cheer leader'. Let yourself and them know how much you believe in them and compliment the person for doing well or their best. (This is dedicated to you Mom for doing your best every day in physical therapy. This is also dedicated to you Dad for helping Mom make it through each day.) Thank you both for showing me and the world how to be someone's 'biggest cheer leader'. Isaiah 35:1-2

Day 361

Forgive yourself for any perceived 'mistakes' you may think you have made on your journey called Life. Believe that Life loves you on every level and everything works out beautifully, similar to the etches and folding of a dove's tail. Luke 3:21-22

Day 362

Every moment of our Lives we have the distinct opportunity to offer up gratitude for all of the goodness we have and continue to receive. An appreciative heart attracts more circumstances, situations and events to be appreciative of. Ezra 3:11

Day 363

Wow! Time flies by quickly, I am on Day 363 of this precious book. I am sending Unshakable Love to each and every word of this book so that as you (my precious reader) reads the pages, the ultimate power of God, which I like to refer to on occasion as Unshakable Love, fills your heart with Love, Happiness, Joy, Great Health, Great Wealth and a generous and kind heart. Psalm 7:17

Day 364

Write, dance, sing, create. The world is awaiting your talent, beauty and beautiful voice. Psalm 89:1

Day 365

Live fully in each moment, show up in the conversation, be a great listener, be your own best friend . Then, you shall notice how true friends and true love appear in your life, finding you and not you pursuing them. Psalm 63:1-11

I am honored to have had the opportunity to share these words with you. My prayer of gratitude consists of me thanking God/Unshakable Love in advance for granting each and everyone of you reading, viewing or listening to this book, A Completely Incredible, Lovely, Wonderful, Spectacular, Absolutely Fabulous Life on every level!!!!! My wish is for each and every area (nook and cranny) of your life and this wish lasts for all eternity, it never expires and the best thing is that all <u>you need</u> to do is take it in like a warm ray of sunshine or like a breath of fresh air. Go in peace my friends and live Your most Excellent Life!!!!

She aspires to creating Inspirational Speaking Workshops and Seminars for individuals , schools and organizations interested in creating the positive lives they desire. Workshops and Seminars may be held via Zoom within the US or abroad.

Ann Marie was born in Boston, Massachusetts and now resides in the Midwest on a small hobby farm, appreciating the beauty of nature and the privilege of breathing in clean crisp fresh air.

She loves art, in particular the Impressionist Period, loves to read, write, paint, sew, knit and partake in nature walks at home and abroad. She has a deep fondness for bottlenose dolphins and Humpback Whales and thrilled when witnessing both on ocean tours.

Feel free to sign up for Workshops or Seminars by sending a message to her Authors page at Balboapress.com

Printed in the United States
by Baker & Taylor Publisher Services